SCREWED

Also by Thom Hartmann

SCREWED

THE UNDECLARED WAR
Against the Middle Class

— And What We Can Do About It

THOM HARTMANN

BERRETT-KOEHLER PUBLISHERS, INC.
San Francisco
a BK Currents book

Berrett-Koehler Publishers, Inc.
235 Montgomery Street, Suite 650
San Francisco, CA 94104-2916
Tel: (415) 288-0260   Fax: (415) 362-2512   www.bkconnection.com

ORDERING INFORMATION

Quantity sales. Special discounts are available on quantity purchases by corporations, associations, and others. For details, contact the "Special Sales Department" at the Berrett-Koehler address above.

Individual sales. Berrett-Koehler publications are available through most bookstores. They can also be ordered directly from Berrett-Koehler: Tel: (800) 929-2929; Fax: (802) 864-7626; www.bkconnection.com

Orders for college textbook/course adoption use. Please contact Berrett-Koehler: Tel: (800) 929-2929; Fax: (802) 864-7626.

Orders by U.S. trade bookstores and wholesalers. Please contact Ingram Publisher Services, Tel: (800) 509-4887; Fax: (800) 838-1149; E-mail: customer.service@ingrampublisherservices.com; or visit www.ingrampublisherservices.com/Ordering for details about electronic ordering.

Berrett-Koehler and the BK logo are registered trademarks of Berrett-Koehler Publishers, Inc.

Printed in the United States of America

Berrett-Koehler books are printed on long-lasting acid-free paper. When it is available, we choose paper that has been manufactured by environmentally responsible processes. These may include using trees grown in sustainable forests, incorporating recycled paper, minimizing chlorine in bleaching, or recycling the energy produced at the paper mill.

Library of Congress Cataloging-in-Publication Data
Hartmann, Thom, 1951–
    Screwed : the undeclared war against the middle class—and what we can
do about it / by Thom Hartmann.— 1st ed.
        p. cm.
    Includes index.
        ISBN: 978-1-57675-414-6   (hardcover)
        ISBN: 978-1-57675-463-4   (paperback)
        1. Middle class—United States—Economic conditions. 2. Middle class—United
    States—Political activity. 3. Middle class—United States—History. 4. United
    States—Social conditions. 5. United States—Politics and government. I. Title.
    Undeclared war against the middle class—and what we can do about it. II. Title.
    HT690.U6H37 2006
    305.5'50973—dc22   2006008003

First Edition

11   10   09   10   9   8   7   6   5   4

Interior design and composition by Gary Palmatier, Ideas to Images.
Elizabeth von Radics, copyeditor; Mike Mollett, proofreader; Edwin Durbin, indexer.

In memory of Carl T. Hartmann,
the world's best dad and the finest
human being I've ever known.

1928–2006

CONTENTS

FOREWORD

Mark Crispin Miller

Here's a bit of wisdom on which "left" and "right" can easily agree: If you let things go, you'll have to pay for it eventually; and the longer you don't deal with it, the more you'll have to pay. Wait long enough, and you'll pay dearly—when you could have done the right thing all along and at little cost.

Take the planet, for example. As every reasonable person and/or group will now admit, this Earth had been gradually heating up since heavy industry began to blacken and enrich the West not long after our founding revolution; and now that trend, for years denied, has started to accelerate, with ever-larger chunks of polar "permafrost" dissolving into sea, polar bears and penguins vanishing, floodwaters rising everywhere, and the weather going mad. Although for decades the danger was strenuously veiled by lots of corporate and religious propaganda, it's now a major story sold dramatically by *Time*, CNN, and Hollywood—and an issue of increasing worry even to Shell Oil, General Motors, and a sizeable network of rational evangelicals. If we had been allowed to face the facts not long ago, when scientists first started trying to talk about them, we might not be wondering now how many species have a future here.

"Global warming" is, at last, a major story, as an overt catastrophe must always be a major story. When it is actually upon us, first of all, there's no denying it (unless you're working in the Bush administration); and, of course, it offers just the sort of stark apocalyptic images that no news outlet can resist (unless they come from places where the scourge in question is our military). Other kinds of long decline are not so mesmerizing—and therefore get no press—although they're just as ruinous as ecological destruction (and are in fact inseparable from it).

Just as we have let the world—and America with it—heat up and otherwise become more poisonous, so have we let things degrade in the civic sphere. Through a sort of continental drift, we have been gradually estranged from our own revolutionary heritage, which these days seems to twinkle dimly at us from the history of some other, better country. That country was a rough republic, where you could either stand up as a citizen or cherish and pursue the right to become one. Ultimately, in that promising republic all were constitutionally free to speak and think and worship as they chose. They were able and inclined to run their government, which had been meticulously structured so as never to devolve into autocracy or oligarchy or mobocracy or any other kind of tyranny. That republic was, or clearly promised to become, "government of the people, by the people, for the people." This was not mere soaring rhetoric or a prosaic cliché but an ideal both humane and rational and, it is now clear, the *only* way that we the people will not perish from the Earth (and take the planet with us when we go).

How did America become the place it is today—a quasi-gulag of bright shopping malls and hidden torture chambers, of crumbling schools and sprawling private jails? How did Americans become a people who could let that happen even though, as this fine book makes clear, it has done them nothing but harm? The change did not, of course, occur when Bush & Co. took over but gradually overcame us through the Civil War, the World Wars, and especially the Cold War and then through the Great Leap Backward that began in earnest when the Cold War ended and the "Red Menace" so rudely disappeared.

To grasp that change, in short, would be to comprehend our entire history; but certainly one major reason for the breakdown is the great blackout on our own revolutionary origins and founding ideology. We have too long denied, and have too long been denied, the truth of what America is really all about.

This revisionary process was already under way when the republic was still in its infancy, with the construction of that dazzling apolitical mythology that still impairs our understanding of American history: That our revolution was made *not* by common men and women sacrificing for the common good but, more attractively (and calmly), by the revered "Founding Fathers," of whom the most paternal was George Washington, "the Father of his Country," as if "we the people" were not self-created and self-ruling but merely his glad and grateful child; that, despite the crucial influence of *Common Sense,* Tom Paine was somehow *not* a "Founding Father"; that those Founders thought and worked in noble unison, all of them in vague agreement as to basic principles. Such misconceptions were already gaining ground while the United States was still authentically (if far from perfectly) republican. And then there were the later prettifying myths of a great national consensus—even more preposterous yet which we all picked up in grammar school—suggesting that the "Founders" were not merely in agreement with each other but somehow agreed also with "the Puritans" who founded the colonial theocracies, as if the United States were *not* a highly radical experiment in atheistic government.

That the early revolutionaries were at odds with one another and that their thinking tended to be highly radical are facts of history that have been whited-out not just by the Establishment. By and large, the left has also minimized our revolutionary heritage although, of course, for very different reasons. In many leftist eyes, America's revolutionaries were not really *revolutionaries,* as that term has long since been romanticized by close association with the Bastille and the Jacobins, the Bolsheviks, *The Sayings of Chairman Mao,* and the hairy, handsome face of Che Guevara.

Having largely bought the soporific mythos of the "Founding Fathers," many leftists have shrugged off our revolution as too stolid and bourgeois to merit any emulation; and, somewhat more understandably, they have condemned the Framers for their tolerance of slavery, for the Indian genocide, and, no less, for having been white Anglo-Saxon males. Thus have U.S. leftists looked primarily to Europe for their intellectual paradigms, relying infinitely more on Marx and Gramsci than on Paine and Jefferson, and otherwise ignoring the unprecedented fire that once lit up the world from our own soil. They have made the grave mistake of seeing slavery and the genocide as so much evidence against the Bill of Rights, when those atrocities prove only that those rights were not revered *enough* by the Americans of yesteryear.

Today the thrilling old duality of "left" and "right" appears increasingly irrelevant—now that the Cold War is a memory—and less meaningful with every passing day as we Americans once more face off against the same ferocious atavistic forces that the Constitution was intended to contain, or thwart, forever: the power-lust of those who would be king, the greed of those who wish they were aristocrats, and the relentless malice of those priesthoods that would force their creed on everybody else. The luminaries of our revolution understood those dangers thoroughly and knew how best to keep them from subverting proper government and making people mostly miserable.

In short, the time has come for us to turn to them again and once more study both their work and their example. For guidance as we thus try to re-educate ourselves, we certainly can do no better than to read Thom Hartmann, whose understanding of our revolutionary heritage, and whose ability to make that understanding clear, is unsurpassed. If you are one who longs to see this nation once again great with promise, this book will enlighten you—and brace you for the necessary fight.

INTRODUCTION

Profits before People

THE STORY OF CARL

Carl loved books and he loved history. After spending two years in the army as part of the American occupation forces in Japan immediately after World War II, Carl was hoping to graduate from college and teach history—perhaps even at the university level—if he could hang on to the GI Bill and his day job long enough to get his PhD. But in 1950, when he'd been married just a few months, the surprise came that forced him to drop out of college: his wife was pregnant with their first child.

This was an era when husbands worked, wives tended the home, and being a good father and provider was one of the highest callings to which a man could aspire. Carl dropped out of school, kept his 9-to-5 job at a camera shop, and got a second job at a metal fabricating plant, working with molten metal from 7:00 p.m. to 4:00 a.m. For much of his wife's pregnancy and his newborn son's first year, he slept three hours a night and caught up on the weekends, but in the process he earned enough to get them an apartment and prepare for the costs of raising a family. Over the next forty-five years, he continued to work in the steel and machine industry, in the later years as a bookkeeper/manager for a Michigan tool-and-die company as three more sons were born.

Carl knew he was doing the right thing when he took that job in the factory, and he did it enthusiastically. Because the auto industry was unionized, he found he was able to support his entire family—all four sons—on one paycheck. He had fully funded health insurance, an annual vacation, and a good pension waiting for him when he retired. Carl had become a member of the middle class. He may not have achieved his personal dream of teaching history, but he had achieved the American dream. He was self-sufficient and free.

Working with molten metal could be dangerous, but the dangers were apparent, and Carl took every precaution to protect himself so that he could return home safe to his family. What he didn't realize, however, was that the asbestos used at the casting operation was an insidious poison. He didn't realize that the asbestos industry had known for decades that the stuff could kill but would continue to profitably market it for another twenty years while actively using its financial muscle to keep the general public in the dark and prevent the government from interfering.

A couple of years ago, Carl tripped on the stairs and ended up in the hospital with a compression fracture of his spine. He figured that fall also caused the terrible pain he'd been experiencing in his abdomen. The doctors, however, discovered that his lungs were filled with mesothelioma, a rare form of lung cancer that is almost always caused by exposure to asbestos. Mesothelioma is terminal, and its victims die by slow and painful suffocation.

Just because some corporation put profit before people, Carl got screwed.

I was Carl's first child.

An Undeclared War

My dad faced a painful death, but at least his job in a union shop left him with health care after retirement. Most Americans don't even have that reassurance anymore. More than 45 million Americans don't have health insurance to cover expenses for a serious illness; 5 million have lost their health insurance in the past four years alone. And it's not just illness that worries most Americans today. Americans are working more and making less. It's getting harder and harder to just get by.

There's a reason for the pain Americans are suffering.

The America my dad grew up in put people before profits. The America he lives in now puts profits before people.

In my dad's America, 35 percent of working people were union members who got a living wage, health insurance, and defined-benefits pensions. These union benefits lifted all boats because they set the floor for employment; for every union job, there was typically a nonunion job with similar pay and benefits (meaning roughly 70 percent of the American workforce back then could raise a family on a single paycheck). People who were disabled and couldn't work could live on Social Security payments, and the elderly knew they would have a safe retirement, paid for by pensions, Social Security, and Medicare. The gap between the richest and the poorest shrunk rather than widened.

That America is disappearing fast. The minimum wage—just $5.15 per hour—is not a living wage. Workers are now expected to pay for their own health insurance and their own retirement. Pension plans are disappearing—30,000 General Motors employees lost theirs in 2005—and there's continued talk of privatizing Social Security. The safety net is ripping apart, and the results are that the middle class is shrinking. The rich are once again getting richer, and the poor are getting poorer:

▶ The inflation-adjusted average annual pay of a CEO went up from $7,773,000 to $9,600,000 from 2002 to 2004. Meanwhile, from 2000 to 2004, the inflation-adjusted median annual household income went down from $46,058 to $44,389. In other words, ordinary people's income went *down* by $1,669 while CEO pay went up by $1,827,000.[1]

▶ Over the past four years, from 2001 to 2005, America has lost 2,818,000 manufacturing jobs. If you don't count jobs produced by the military-industrial complex, the number of private sector jobs created since 2001 has *decreased* by 1,160,000.[2]

▶ Although 67 percent of large employers (more than 500 employees) offer a traditional pension, that is down from 91 percent two decades ago, and it's dropping fast as more companies freeze pensions and turn instead to 401(k)s.[3] Only 6 percent of Americans working in the private sector can rely on a defined pension,[4] and 76 percent of Baby Boomers say they don't think they are very prepared to meet their retirement expenses.[5]

▶ Today only 60 percent of employers provide health care to their employees. More than 45 million Americans were without health insurance as of 2004, and we can only guess that that number has grown.[6]

You don't need the numbers because you probably already know someone who has been forced out of the middle class. Roger, for instance, who once was a vice president of research and development for a software engineering company, lost his job during the dot-com bust and never got it back. After being unemployed for seven years, he's thinking of getting a job as a "landscape engineer"—that's a gardener—at a tenth of his former salary.

Or there's the case of Bob, a college graduate who has been holding three jobs for the past five years, one full-time as a bookstore clerk, two part-time. Even though he works sixty hours a week, he doesn't make enough money to rent his own apartment (he rents a room in a shared flat) and he can't afford health insurance. He hopes his allergies don't turn into asthma because he can't afford the medication he would need for that.

Too many Americans are just holding on. Consider Amy: Divorced from her alcoholic husband, she has gone back to school full-time to become a teacher; she earns a living by catering on the weekends. A single mother, she and her daughter share a studio apartment. Amy has neither health insurance nor child care and no nearby relatives—she relies on neighbors to take care of her daughter. One major illness and Amy would be homeless.

And then there are most of the rest of us, who have good jobs but still don't feel secure about the future. Ralph and Sally both get health insurance through their jobs, but their mortgage eats up more than 60 percent of their income, and the clothes and the necessities they buy for their two kids consume whatever might be left after groceries and utilities. They have health insurance but no pension. Their retirement is based on the few thousand dollars a year they can put into their IRAs. They wonder how they will be able to send their kids to college and afford to retire.

Today a man like my dad couldn't support a family of six on one paycheck. The middle class my dad belonged to is on its deathbed. Meanwhile, sitting around the pool, waiting for the dividend checks to roll in (while paying a maximum 15 percent income tax), the corporate class grows even wealthier.

How can this be?

How is it that companies could sell asbestos when they knew it would kill people? Why do people go hungry in America, the world's wealthiest nation? Why is it that people like you and me who work long, full days cannot afford to get sick, cannot buy houses, and cannot send their kids to college? What's happened to the middle class?

These questions are about our economy, but the answer is about who we are as a country.

DEMOCRACY AND THE MIDDLE CLASS

The most ancient form of democracy is found among virtually all indigenous peoples of the world. It's the way humans have lived for more than 150,000 years. There are no rich and no poor among most tribal people—everybody is "middle class." There is also little hierarchy. The concept of "chief" is one that Europeans brought with them to America—which in large part is what produced so much confusion in the 1600s and 1700s in America as most Native American tribes would never delegate absolute authority to any one person to sign a treaty. Instead decisions were made by consensus in these most ancient cauldrons of democracy.

The Founders of this nation, and the Framers of our Constitution, were heavily influenced and inspired by the democracy they saw all around them. Much of the U.S. Constitution is based on the Iroquois Confederacy—the five (later six) tribes who occupied territories from New England to the edge of the Midwest. It was a democracy with elected representatives, an upper and lower house, and a supreme court (made up entirely of women, who held final say in five of the six tribes).

As Benjamin Franklin noted to his contemporaries at the Constitutional Convention: "It would be a very strange thing if Six Nations of Ignorant Savages should be capable of forming a Scheme for such an Union and be able to execute it in such a manner, as that it has subsisted Ages, and appears indissoluble, and yet a like union should be impracticable for ten or a dozen English colonies."

The Framers modeled the oldest democracies, and the oldest forms of the middle class, and thus helped create the truly widespread and strong first middle class in the history of modern civilization.

Back in Europe, however, the sort of democracy the Framers were borrowing and inventing, and even the existence of a middle class itself, was considered unnatural. For most of the seven thousand years of recorded human history, all the way back to the *Gilgamesh Epic*, the oldest written story, what we call a middle class is virtually unheard of—as was democracy. Throughout most of the history of what we call civilization, an unrestrained economy and the idea of hierarchical social organization has always produced a small ruling elite and a large number of nearly impoverished workers.

Up until the founding of America, the middle class was considered unnatural by many political philosophers. Thomas Hobbes wrote in his 1651 magnum opus *Leviathan* that the world was better off with the rule of the few over the many, even if that meant that the many were impoverished. Without a strong and iron-fisted ruler, Hobbes wrote, there would be "no place for industry . . . no arts, no letters, no society." Because Hobbes believed that ordinary people couldn't govern themselves, he believed that most people would be happy to exchange personal freedom and economic opportunity for the ability to live in safety and security. For the working class to have both freedom *and* security, Hobbes suggested, was impossible.

Our nation's Founders disagreed. They believed in the rights of ordinary people to self-determination, so they created a form of government where We the People rule. They declared that all people, and not just the elite, have the right to "life, liberty, and the pursuit of happiness." (In that declaration, Thomas Jefferson replaced John Locke's famous "life, liberty, and property" with "life, liberty, and *happiness*"—the first time the word had ever appeared in the founding document of any nation.) They believed that We the People could create a country founded on personal freedom and economic opportunity for all. The Founders believed in the power of a middle class; and in defiance of Hobbes and the conventional wisdom of Europe, they believed that democracy and a middle class were the "natural state of man."

As John Quincy Adams argued before the Supreme Court in 1841 on behalf of freeing rebelling slaves in the Amistad case, he stood before and pointed to a copy of the Declaration of Independence:

> That DECLARATION says that every man is "endowed by his Creator with certain inalienable rights," and that "among

these are life, liberty, and the pursuit of happiness.". . . I will not here discuss the right or the rights of slavery, but I say that the doctrine of Hobbes, that War is the natural state of man, has for ages been exploded, as equally disclaimed and rejected by the philosopher and the Christian. That it is utterly incompatible with any theory of human rights, and especially with the rights which the Declaration of Independence proclaims as self-evident truths.

It turns out that the Founders knew something Hobbes didn't know: political democracy and an economic middle class is the natural state of humankind. Indeed, it's the natural state of the entire animal kingdom.

For example, biologists used to think that animal societies were ruled by alpha males. Recent studies, however, have found that while it's true that alpha males (and females, in some species) have the advantage in courtship rituals, that's where their power ends. Biologists Tim Roper and L. Conradt discovered that animals don't follow a leader but instead move together.[7]

James Randerson did a follow-up study with red deer to prove the point.[8] How does a herd of deer decide it's time to stop grazing and go toward the watering hole? As they're grazing, various deer point their bodies in seemingly random directions, until it comes time to go drink. Then individuals begin to graze while facing one of several watering holes. When a majority of deer are pointing toward one particular watering hole, they all move in that direction. Randerson saw instances where the alpha deer was actually one of the last to move toward the hole rather than one of the first.

When I interviewed Tim Roper about his research at the University of Sussex in the United Kingdom, he told me that when his findings were first published, scientists from all over the world called to tell him that they were seeing the same thing with their research subjects. Birds flying in flocks aren't following a leader but monitoring the motions of those around them for variations in the flight path; when more than 50 percent have moved in a particular direction—even if it's only a quarter-inch in one direction or another—the entire flock "suddenly" veers off that way. It's the same with fish and even with swarms of gnats. Roper said that his colleagues were telling him that from ants to gorillas, democracy is the norm among animals. Just like with indigenous human societies—which have had hundreds of thousands of years of trial and error to work out the best ways to live—democracy is the norm among animals, and (other than for the Darwinian purpose of finding the best mate) hierarchy/kingdom is the rarity.

Thus, we discover, this close relationship between the middle class and democracy is burned into our DNA—along with that of the entire animal kingdom (an ironic term, given this new information). In a democracy there may be an elite (like the alpha male deer), but they don't rule the others. Instead the group is ruled by the vast middle—what in economic terms we would call a middle class.

A true democracy both produces a middle class and requires a middle class for survival. Like the twin strands of DNA, democracy and the middle class are inextricably intertwined, and to break either is to destroy the viability of both.

In human society as well, to have a democracy we must have a middle class. And to have a true middle class, a majority of the people in a nation must be educated and economically secure and must have full and easy access to real news so they can make informed decisions. Democracy requires that its citizens be able to afford to take care of themselves and their families when they get sick, to afford a decent place to live, to find meaningful and well-paying work, and to anticipate—and enjoy—a secure retirement.

This is the American Dream. It's the America my dad grew up in and the America I grew up in. It's the America that is quickly slipping away from us under the burden of crony capitalism and a political system corrupted by it.

When there is no American Dream, when there is no middle class, there cannot be real democracy. That's why when elections are brought to nations that are in crisis or that don't have a broad, stable, well-educated middle class—such as Egypt, Iraq, Iran, and the Palestinian territories—the result is aristocrats, "strongmen," or theocrats exploiting those elections as a way of gaining decidedly undemocratic power.

America's Founders understood the relationship between the middle class—what Thomas Jefferson called the *yeomanry*—and democracy. Jefferson's greatest fear for the young American nation was not a new king but a new economic aristocracy. He worried that if a small group of citizens became too wealthy—if America became polarized between the very rich and the very poor—democracy would vanish.

Our democracy depends upon our ability to play referee to the game of business and to protect labor and the public good. It is both our right and our responsibility, Jefferson insisted, to control "overgrown wealth" from becoming "dangerous to the state"— which is, so long as we are a democratic republic, We the People.

When wealth is concentrated in the hands of the few and the middle class shrinks to the point where it's no longer a politically potent force, democracy becomes a feudal aristocracy—the rule of the elite. As Franklin D. Roosevelt pointed out in 1936, the rule of the many requires that We the People have a degree of economic as well as political freedom. When We the People are given the opportunity to educate ourselves, earn a living wage, own our own homes, and feel confident that we have good child care, health care, and care in our old age—in short, when America has a thriving middle class—America also has a thriving democracy.

Without this strong and vibrant middle class, democracy cannot exist; instead, it becomes a caricature of itself. There are leaders and elections and all the forms, but they're only for show; the game is now rigged.

DEMOCRATS VERSUS THE CONS

There's a battle waging today in America that will decide the future of the middle class. On the one side are those like Thomas Jefferson who believe that a free people can govern themselves and have the right to organize their government to create a strong middle class—which will, in turn, keep the government democratic. On the other side are those like Thomas Hobbes who believe that only a small elite can and should govern and that the people should be willing to pay the price of poverty in exchange for security.

Those who don't want democracy understand that a middle class will always work to create democracy, which is why they are so opposed to middle-class-creating government policies like free public education, limits on the concentration of ownership of the media, and social safety nets like universal health care and Social Security. They understand that such policies have, and always will, bring about a strong and vibrant middle class that will, in turn, both demand and create a more democratic society.

Who are these people who want to undermine the middle class? They often call themselves "conservatives" or "neo-conservatives," but these people are not true conservatives. They don't want to "conserve" or protect the America the Founders gave us. I call them "cons" because they are conning America.

My dad was a staunch Republican all his life, but he didn't believe that a small elite should rule America. He was glad the government provided safety nets like Social Security and Medicare and made unionization possible. My dad, and most of the other *real* conservatives I have known, believed in the middle class and believed in democracy.

The battle we face in America today is not between liberal and conservative, nor is it between big-*D* Democrat and Republican. The battle we face today is between those of us who want to protect our democratic heritage and the cons who want to create an

America that benefits only a small elite organized around corporate power and inherited wealth.

THE CON GAME

Two types of cons have worked together to screw the middle class. Call them the *predator cons* and the *true believer cons.*

Predator Cons

Predator cons are simply greedy. They use politics and/or philosophy as a cover for their theft of our common resources and as a rationalization for their growing wealth in the face of growing societal poverty. They are not conservatives in any true sense—they are not interested in conserving American values or even in keeping American wealth in America. They're the ones who ship jobs overseas, lobby for tax breaks from Congress, fight against the inheritance tax, and reincorporate their companies offshore to avoid paying U.S. corporate taxes.

The predator cons' rationalization for their obscene pileup of wealth is that they're simply playing the game by the existing rules; and that's true to a large extent—except that they're also the ones who bought and paid for the politicians who set up the rules for them. They have conned America into believing that they care about the American economy when all they care about is making money for themselves.

A great example of a predatory con is NAFTA, the North American Free Trade Agreement. These agreements lower wages for American workers—they do not create well-paying jobs in America. They create record trade deficits. Cons don't even try to argue that free-trade agreements are good for America anymore. Agreements like these—such as the Central American Free Trade Agreement (CAFTA)—are passed now (by a single vote in the Senate in 2005) only because corporate America needs them to reap tremendous profits from the low wages they extract in nonunionized, nondemocratic, and socially disorganized countries; predator cons succeed in passing these agreements by threatening to withhold campaign funds from anyone who dares to oppose them.

It's an old game that the robber barons of the nineteenth century knew well how to play.

True Believer Cons

The second type of con is perhaps even more dangerous than the predators. They're the true believers.

Just as true believers in communism brought about the death of tens of millions in Russia from the time of the Bolshevik Revolution until the fall of the Berlin Wall, so too the true believers in laissez faire capitalism believe that if only government would go away, everything would be just fine. Employers would become benevolent, employees would be enthusiastic, and bureaucratic inefficiencies would vanish.

These so-called free marketeers aren't bothered by the consolidation of companies or the loss of competition that happens when markets are unregulated. Like Thomas Hobbes, the true believers assume that society will run best when run by the small elite that comes out on top. They believe in *corporatocracy*—the view that an economic aristocracy benefits the working class because wealth will "trickle down" from above to below.

Ronald Reagan was a true believer. He didn't understand economics, and the simple notions of self-sufficiency and a pioneering spirit appealed to him. He asked, in essence: "Why would somebody want to regulate a business? Wouldn't it eventually always do what was best without regulation?"

What Reagan and his followers failed to understand was that business will *not* always do what's best for society. In fact, the fundamental goal of business—to maximize assets and profits while externalizing costs and liabilities—is often *destructive* to the public good. This becomes particularly obvious when business owners do not live or otherwise participate in the same society and culture as their customers. A small-business owner can't run sewage out his door or pay his workers below a living wage because he has to face his next-door neighbor and his next-door neighbor's kid, who may want to work in his shop.

The same is not true, however, for multinational corporations. Executives of large corporations don't live in the same society as the people who work for them and who live next to their factories. As a result, the legacy of unregulated big business and the concentration of wealth in the hands of the few is pollution, worker exploitation, cuts to worker safety, and the bestowing of profits to the company's elite while cutting benefits to the company's rank and file.

The true believer cons would just be wrong, and not dangerous, if they didn't try to hide their corporatocratic, market-before-people agenda. They have discovered, however, that most people don't agree with them that a government ruled by a small elite is the most stable form of government and that stability and predictability are more important than democracy. Saying this sort of thing out loud loses elections, so these conservatives have learned to con the public by hiding their agenda behind euphemisms and double-speak.

The Bush Jr. administration has perfected the true believer con. Letting a corporate elite control, profit from, and make decisions about our air, water, and sewage systems is called the Clear Skies Initiative and the Clean Water Initiative; or, when they're feeling a bit more open, "privatization." Letting a corporate elite count our votes in secret on their privately owned machines and tell us how we voted is called the Help America Vote Act. Cutting holes in our social safety net programs like Social Security and Medicare is called "strengthening" these programs through increased "consumer-driven choice" and "personal accounts."

Cons suggest that when consumers pool their risk with a private, for-profit corporation to protect personal property, it is called "insurance" and it's a good thing; but when citizens pool their risk with the government to guarantee health care, retirement, and a social safety net, that is "socialism" and should be "privatized." Translated, the cons' policies mean only one thing: you and I get screwed.

Will we choose a society of, by, and for We the People or a society ruled by the cons' corporatocracy? Will we choose to maintain the middle class that has made America a democracy, or will we let the middle class get screwed?

FIGHTING BACK

When cons took over the United States during Reconstruction after the Civil War and held power until the Republican Great Depression, the damage they did was tremendous. Our nation was wracked by the classic scourges of poverty—epidemics of disease, crime, and riots—and the average working person was little more than a serf. The concepts of owning a home, having health or job security, and enjoying old age were unthinkable for all but the mercantile class and the rich. America seemed to be run for the robber barons and not for the thousands who worked for them. Democracy in America was at its lowest ebb; our nation more resembled the Victorian England that Dickens wrote of than the egalitarian and middle-class-driven democracy that Alexis de Tocqueville saw here in 1836.

All that changed in the 1930s, when Franklin D. Roosevelt's New Deal brought back the middle class. His economic stimulus programs put money in people's pockets, and the safety nets he created—like Social Security—ensured that no one would fall out of the middle class once they had gotten there. His programs worked, creating what has been called the Golden Age of the middle class. During these years, from the 1940s until Reagan took power, democracy in America resurged along with the middle class.

But after forty years of prosperity, in the 1980s Americans began drinking the cons' Kool-Aid with startling rapidity. Three "conservative" Republican presidents and one "conservative" Democrat have crushed the middle class and brought our nation to the brink of a second Great Depression.

In 2005 the U.S. trade deficit hit an all-time high at a whopping $725.8 billion. Over the past five years, the U.S. economy has experienced the slowest job creation since the 1930s, with fewer private-sector hours worked in 2005 than in 2001. For the first time since the Great Depression, in 2005 American consumers spent more than they earned, and the government budget deficit was larger than all business savings combined.[9] We are financing today's consumption with tomorrow's bills, and sooner or later the chits will come in and the middle class will be the big losers—putting democracy itself at risk again.

The way out of this mess isn't difficult to understand—we've done it before. Remember that businesses are run like kingdoms, with CEO kings, executive princes, and worker serfs, so they're essentially anti-democratic. Avoiding the cons' scenario simply requires us to remember that a middle class won't emerge when business has more influence in the halls of government than do We the People. Without democracy there can be no middle class; and without a middle class, democracy will wither and die.

Whether our economy benefits billionaires or the rest of us is determined by how we handle economic policy. It depends especially on a fundamental grasp of two concepts: classical economics and an internal government-spending stimulus.

Classical Economics

For more than two hundred years—until Ronald Reagan became president—economics was not hard to understand. Everyone could figure out that when working people have money, they spend most of it. When extremely wealthy people have money, they save most of it. It's the spending of money by working people that creates consumer demand. Consumer demand in turn creates business opportunities, and that creates jobs.

In 1981 Reagan introduced America to *trickle-down economics,* also called (by George H. W. Bush, who understood classical economics even though he later had to placate the con base) "voodoo economics." Reagan's concept, in a nutshell, was that if we reorganized society so that the wealth of the rich grew suddenly and quickly, they'd use that money to build factories and hire more people, thus allowing their wealth to "trickle down" to the workers.

This assertion of Reagan's was new—it had never before happened in the history of the world. Certainly small groups of political and/or economic elites had concentrated wealth at the expense of society generally, but none had ever before said they were doing it because *economics* justified it. Kings throughout history had simply claimed the divine right of kings.

Even though voodoo economics had never been tried, Reagan was able to convince average Americans that it would work, and got it pushed through Congress. (Members of Congress saw it for what it was, but so did their wealthy contributors who would benefit from it, so Republicans and a few sellout "conservative" Democrats in Congress went along.) To institute his voodoo economics, Reagan slashed top marginal income tax rates on millionaires and billionaires from 70 percent to 50 percent in 1981 and all the way down to 28 percent by 1988.[10]

The result wasn't at all what Reagan expected. Rather than create income, the Reagan tax cuts dropped the United States into the greatest debt in the history of the world. Reagan turned to his conservative friend Alan Greenspan, who suggested that Reagan could hide part of the debt by borrowing a few hundred billion dollars a year from the Social Security Trust Fund.[11] Reagan followed Greenspan's advice, which is why we have a Social Security crisis today: the government borrowed all the money in the fund from 1982 to today to help cover the voodoo economics budget deficit; and now, to pay back Social Security, income taxes—which hit millionaires and billionaires (unlike Social Security FICA taxes, which are taken only on the first $90,000 of income from working people)—rose substantially.

Additionally, as would be expected, the rich got fabulously richer under Reagan. From 1980 to 1990, the income of the wealthiest 5 percent of Americans rose by 25 percent while the income of the bottom 40 percent stayed absolutely flat.[12] This is why the most wealthy in America didn't use their money to build factories—after all, there wasn't a significant increase in demand, so why manufacture things that people can't afford? Instead this nation's rich loaned some of their money to the U.S. government so it could pay the bills Reagan was running up, getting it back over the ensuing twenty years with a healthy dose of interest, paid for by future taxpayers.

Although trickle-down economics did produce millions of jobs, they were almost all outside of the United States, while at the same time good U.S. manufacturing jobs vanished. The only accomplishment of trickle-down economics was to produce a nation of peons.

The alternative is to return to classical economics. When working people have money to spend, they create a demand for goods and services, which allows entrepreneurs to start businesses to meet that demand. The entrepreneurs employ more working people, who then have more money to spend. The middle class grows.

Think about it. What would you do if someone gave you an extra $20,000? Maybe you would take a vacation or buy a new car, new clothes, or new appliances. Even if you used the money to pay off old bills, you would then have more to spend in the future because you wouldn't have interest payments. And when you buy more, you create demand, which means more people can be put to work—and the economy grows.

Now think about what Bill Gates would do if someone gave him an extra $20,000—or an extra $20 million or more, as George W. Bush's first tax cuts did. Would he even notice? He'd probably just send it along to his accountant and forget all about it. The only thing that's going to grow is Bill Gates's bank account. That's the difference between giving money to the rich and giving money to you and me.

This economic truth is just common sense. When people in the lower and middle economic layers of society have increased income, all of society eventually gets richer because working people's spending most of their incomes is the engine that creates economic demand for goods and services.

To bring back the middle class, we must reinstitute common-sense classical economics: we must pay a living wage to working people, protect U.S. industries, and reinstate progressive taxation so the very wealthy pay a share of their income that reflects their heavier use of the commons and their increased access to the engines of wealth generation.

Government-spending Stimulus

Our annual savings rate in the United States has recently hit a low of –0.5.[13] You don't usually see a number like that in a book about the modern U.S. economy. That negative number means not only that people aren't saving but that they're spending what savings they have. The last time we saw an annual savings rate in negative numbers like that was in 1933—the trough of the Great Depression.

The unemployment rate has hovered at 4.9 percent, but the government figures don't include "discouraged workers" who want jobs but have stopped looking. When you add that category, you get an unemployment rate of 8.3 percent.[14] That's creeping into dangerous territory. If you considered underemployment in the same category, we'd be back in the Great Depression right now.

So what's keeping the U.S. economy afloat? Turns out, not much.

First, there's personal debt. The American middle class is more in debt than ever before in the history of this nation. While cons like to say "more people own their homes than ever before," that's only true if by "own their homes" you mean "are massively in debt to a bank instead of having a rental contract." Ditto for people "owning their own cars." Add to that the average credit card debt per household, which is now more than 2004's record of $9,312—up a whopping 116 percent over the past 10 years.[15]

In large part this personal debt has been sustained by a single force—the steady increase in the "value" of housing, particularly since Alan Greenspan threw interest rates into negative territory in 2003–2004 to help George W. Bush get reelected. People refinanced their homes, "extracted equity," and spent it as if it were income—fueling consumer demand and keeping the economy afloat. But as a result, Americans are now deeper in debt than ever, and many with adjustable-rate or interest-only mortgages are being wiped out as interest rates rise back up into normal territory.

While increasing personal debt has accounted for some of the appearance of a stable American economy, a much larger factor has been government borrowing and war spending. In 2005 the Bush administration was borrowing more than $2 billion per day—and spending nearly all of it back into the U.S. economy. This spending—a good chunk of it going to cronies of Bush and Cheney for rebuilding Iraq and New Orleans—provided a cosmetic stimulus that helped make the economy appear to be working. It was similar to how the family next door might seem like they're living large—until you discover they're $60,000 in debt on twenty different credit cards. In the case of our nation, Bush Jr.'s credit card bill is for more than $4,000 billion ($4,000,000,000,000), on top of Reagan's and Bush Sr.'s $3 trillion debt—a bill that will be paid by our children and our grandchildren.

One of the most tragic parts of Bush Jr.'s borrowed-money government-spending stimulus was that it was for defense spending. Although FDR used deficit spending (albeit a fraction of what Reagan or Bush has done) to finance such New Deal enterprises as the Works Projects Administration (WPA), he used that money to build core parts of America's infrastructure—roads, bridges, dams, reforestation, urban reconstruction, and water and sewage systems. Much of it is still producing a return on investment more than seventy years later. Bush's spending, however, leaves only soldiers with post-traumatic stress disorder, a depleted-uranium-contaminated wasteland in the Middle East, and a few dozen fat cats in the defense industry.

Government spending can be used to rebuild the middle class. When government builds a bridge or a school or a water treatment plant, that infrastructure strengthens communities and lasts for generations, providing a continuous and growing return on the initial investment. Government can invest in jobs, providing workers with good wages that they will reinvest in consumer goods. Government can provide workers with a social safety net and with high-quality public education that will help them climb out of poverty and into the middle class. Government can regulate business, creating a level playing field for workers. It worked well between 1935 and 1981, and it could work again.

Along with increasing personal debt and a deepening government-spending deficit, the American economy has been pushed by a growing trade deficit (also known as the "balance of payments" debt). In 2005 we bought more than $700 billion more in goods and services from other countries than we sold (and more than $200 billion of that was just with China!). We've been doing this pretty constantly ever since the mid-Reagan years, when he began hollowing out the core of American manufacturing, a process that kicked into warp speed when Bill Clinton pushed through and signed NAFTA and the General Agreement on Tariffs and Trade (GATT).

The result is that countries all over the world are sitting on dollars we've paid them for things we bought, but they don't want to buy anything back from us because we no longer manufacture TVs or computers or shoes or much of anything. So what do they do with the money? They buy us. They buy our remaining manufacturing companies, our ports, our banks, our forests, our landmark buildings, and our real estate. Chrysler is gone, as is John

Hancock Insurance. Ditto for Wells Fargo Bank and what was the Helmsley Building in New York.

Reagan, Bush Sr., Clinton, and Bush Jr.—and twenty-five years of a largely "conservative" (that is, "con") Congress—have quite literally sold off America in exchange for enough money to keep on buying consumer junk to stock the shelves of Wal-Mart and other "value" retailers of foreign goods.

The nonprofit www.EconomyInCrisis.org offers figures compiled from IRS tax returns that show that large chunks of "America" are no longer owned by Americans (see the list on pages 23–24).

Cons call this "insourcing" and tell us it's a good thing. "Toyota is giving Americans jobs by building factories here!" they shout with a smile as they give Toyota another huge tax break (paid for by its workers) to site a factory. "Your company has been bought by the Saudis and the ports are owned by the British, but your paycheck is still just as good!" they reassure us.

But there's a reason why companies do business: to make a profit. And when the company is an American company, that profit typically stays in America, where it's used to build more factories or buy more advertising or pay better salaries. It contributes to economic growth. It keeps going around and around in our economy, getting taxed in each cycle and thus providing for good schools, safer roads, and decent salaries for our cops and firefighters.

When foreign-owned companies do business in America, however, they do so with the express purpose of taking their profits home. Paine Webber's profits now go to Switzerland, Amoco's go to the United Kingdom, and Transamerica's go to the Netherlands. Chrysler's profits go to Germany; ditto for Random House's and Westinghouse's.

The con has gone global and is even now starting to hit some western European countries that have been seduced by the so-called free-trade sales pitch for increased corporate power and decreased citizens' rights.

Percentage of Foreign Ownership of Specific U.S. Industries

- ► Sound-recording industries   97%
- ► Commodity contracts dealing and brokerage   79%
- ► Motion picture and sound-recording industries   75%
- ► Metal ore mining   65%
- ► Motion picture and video industries   64%
- ► Wineries and distilleries   64%
- ► Database, directory, and other publishers   63%
- ► Book publishers   63%
- ► Cement, concrete, lime, and gypsum products   62%
- ► Engine, turbine, and power transmission equipment   57%
- ► Rubber products   53%
- ► Nonmetallic mineral product manufacturing   53%
- ► Plastics and rubber products manufacturing   52%
- ► Plastics products   51%
- ► Other insurance-related activities   51%
- ► Boiler, tank, and shipping containers   50%
- ► Glass and glass products   48%
- ► Coal mining   48%
- ► Sugar and confectionery products   48%
- ► Nonmetallic mineral mining and quarrying   47%
- ► Advertising and related services   41%
- ► Pharmaceutical and medicine   40%
- ► Clay, refractory, and other nonmetallic mineral products   40%
- ► Securities brokerage   38%
- ► Other general-purpose machinery   37%
- ► Audio and video equipment manufacturing and reproducing magnetic and optical media   36%
- ► Support activities for mining   36%
- ► Soap, cleaning compound, and toilet preparation   32%

Foreign Ownership of U.S. Industries *(continued)*

- ► Chemical manufacturing   30%
- ► Industrial machinery   30%
- ► Securities, commodity contracts, and other financial investments and related activities   30%
- ► Other food   29%
- ► Motor vehicles and parts   29%
- ► Machinery manufacturing   28%
- ► Other electrical equipment and components   28%
- ► Securities and commodity exchanges and other financial investment activities   27%
- ► Architectural, engineering, and related services   26%
- ► Credit card issuing and other consumer credit   26%
- ► Petroleum refineries (including integrated)   25%
- ► Navigational, measuring, electromedical, and control instruments   25%
- ► Petroleum and coal products manufacturing   25%
- ► Transportation equipment manufacturing   25%
- ► Commercial and service industry machinery   25%
- ► Basic chemicals   24%
- ► Investment banking and securities dealing   24%
- ► Semiconductor and other electronic components   23%
- ► Paint, coatings, and adhesives   22%
- ► Printing and related support activities   21%
- ► Chemical product and preparation   20%
- ► Iron, steel mills, and steel products   20%
- ► Agriculture, construction, and mining machinery   20%
- ► Publishing industries   20%
- ► Medical equipment and supplies   20%

Source: www.economyincrisis.org/congress/foreignownedind.asp (accessed March 25, 2006).

But it really began in full force here, with Reagan, Bush Sr., and Clinton, and here is where its fruits are most obvious. For more than two hundred years, America was the wealthiest and most powerful nation in the world. Today—after nearly three decades of the cons' economics and insane "free-trade" policies—we're the most indebted nation in the history of the world.

We've gone from being—pre-Reagan—the world's largest exporter of finished goods and the world's largest importer of raw materials to being—just over the past decade—the exact opposite. We used to import iron ore, make steel, make cars, and export them all around the world. Now Canadian and Mexican and German companies mine raw materials from mines they own in the United States, ship the ore to their nations or to China, manufacture the finished goods, and sell those goods back to us—with dollars we give them in exchange for another few hundred billion dollars' worth of America every year.

There's no reason to let the cons screw us over. We must not stand by while our democracy becomes a corporatocracy, serving an elite group of billionaire CEOs. There is another way—and we've done it before. Thomas Jefferson knew how to build a middle class. Franklin Roosevelt knew how. We can do it, too. We can re-create the America that built the middle class my dad entered, the middle class in which he raised me.

PART I

A Middle Class Requires Democracy

Every year at Christmastime, millions of Americans watch TV portrayals of Charles Dickens's classic novel *A Christmas Carol*. In the story a regular guy named Bob Cratchit works at the firm of Scrooge and Marley.

Bob works full-time, plus nights and weekends, but even so he has no idea how he'll be able to afford Christmas dinner let alone gifts for his children. He can't afford medical care for his son, dooming Tiny Tim to either death or a lifetime deformity. He puts up with daily abuse from his employer because he lives in terror of unemployment and homelessness.

Bob Cratchit is screwed.

We like watching *A Christmas Carol* because Bob's boss, Ebenezer Scrooge, famously has a change of heart and "donates" Christmas dinner to the Cratchit family as well as health care for Tiny Tim. Yet as we watch the show, we often forget the subtext of the story: without strong worker protections and/or unions, the workplace is not a democracy—it more closely resembles a kingdom, and the worker is the "property" of the employer. (Dickens knew this well—his own father was once thrown into debtor's prison.)

In the seven-thousand-year history of the "civilized" world, most regular folks have been like Bob Cratchit.

Because the history of "civilization" is the history of anti-democratic kings and kingdoms (or theocrats or other despots), most of the average people over the past seven thousand years in "civilized" countries either have been slaves or, if workers like Cratchit, have worked as hard as they could and still had trouble getting by.

For virtually all of recorded history, society has been divided into a small but fabulously wealthy ownership class (who were also the political rulers) and a large but poor slave, serf, and/or working class. Because of this lack of democracy—both in government and in the workplace (a union is democracy in the workplace)—outside of a small mercantilist class and a very few skilled tradesmen who managed to organize into guilds, a middle class has been an aberration.

A middle class can't exist when democracy is weak or absent. It arises only when We the People have a strong say in both our government and our workplace.

CHAPTER 1

There Is No
"Free" Market

Look at history and you will find that the middle class was the creation of liberal democracies. George Washington and Thomas Jefferson did not fight a bloody war to create a country only for wealthy property holders. (See chapter 4 to fully understand how wrong is the corrosive myth of the "rich Founders.") Our Founders believed that every Bob Cratchit willing to work for his living should be able to earn enough to own his house and support himself and his family. That's what it means to be middle class—and part of why Jefferson put "life, liberty and the pursuit of happiness" into the Declaration of Independence.

The Founders also knew that the middle class doesn't just materialize out of thin air. That's why, in the preamble to the Constitution, they wrote that one purpose of government was to "promote the general welfare."

Two centuries later, when the middle class was in danger of disappearing during the Great Depression, Franklin D. Roosevelt almost single-handedly created a new middle class through his New Deal policies. Roosevelt's success demonstrates that government can and must "promote the general welfare" because only government can create the conditions that make a middle class possible. And FDR was able to do it only because an overwhelming majority of Americans voted for it in a relatively free and open democracy.

THE LIE OF THE "FREE" MARKET

Listen to the right-wing pundits—the people I call the *cons*—and they will tell you something completely different. They suggest (and some actually believe) that a middle class will naturally spring into being when the kingdoms of corporate power are freed from government restrictions.

The way to create good jobs, according to the cons, is to "free" the market. When business gets to do whatever it wants, they say, it will create wealth, and that wealth will trickle down to the rest of us, creating a middle class.

The cons' belief in "free" markets is a bit like the old Catholic Church's insistence that the Earth was at the center of the solar system. The free-market line is widely believed by those in power, and those who challenge this belief are labeled heretics—and it's wrong.

Here's a headline for these cons who are masquerading as economists without having studied either economics or history:

There is no such thing as a "free" market.
Markets are the creation of government.

Governments provide markets with a stable currency for financial transactions. They provide a legal infrastructure and a court system to enforce the contracts that make the market possible. They provide an educated workforce through public education, and those workers show up at their places of business after traveling on public roads, rails, and airways provided by the government. Businesses that use the "free" market are protected by police and fire departments provided by the government, and they send their communications—from phone to e-mail—over lines that follow public rights of way maintained and protected by the government.

And, most important, the rules of the game of business are defined by the government. Any sports fan can tell you that without rules and referees football, baseball, basketball, and hockey would be a mess. Similarly, business without rules won't work. In a corporate kingdom—a *corporatocracy*—those rules are made by the businesses themselves and will inevitably screw workers and citizens. In a democracy those rules are made by We the People, both through our elected representatives and through union negotiations with the business kings/lords/CEOs.

THE "SMALLER-GOVERNMENT" CON

The cons believe that what business does is business's business and that government should keep its nose out of it, even when the business is run by Ebenezer Scrooge and leads to centuries of sick Tiny Tims and terrified Bob Cratchits.

Talk-show cons and TV talking-head cons and political cons—both Republicans and "conservative" or "middle of the road" (euphemisms for *corporate connected*) Democrats—say that government just gets in the way of the market. They want to "let the market decide" our economy.

Unspoken is their belief that if economic and social policy are made by the market, we don't need government—the voice and the will of We the People—for most domestic affairs. One of the most vocal cons, Grover Norquist, told National Public Radio's Mara Liasson in a May 25, 2001, interview, "I don't want to abolish government. I simply want to reduce it to the size where I can drag it into the bathroom and drown it in the bathtub."

During the Golden Age of the American middle class, people routinely voted themselves tax increases to invest in new schools, better roads, higher pay for police and firefighters, and a multitude of other infrastructure and public works projects. Hospitals were owned and run by local communities, as were water and sewage systems and, in most of the United States, power plants and other public utilities. Taxes by and large were thought of as investments in civil society and community and were routinely embraced by the majority of the middle class. Of course, people made jokes about not liking taxes, but they still knew that without taxes there would be no services, and people wanted and needed those services.

Ronald Reagan and his public relations (PR) machine, funded by huge corporations and wealthy people like Joseph Coors, promoted the thought virus—the meme—that taxes are bad and government is bad. Reagan ran as an "outsider" to government (although he was the former governor of California) and even ran for reelection as president "against" government.

Reagan put forward the point of view of the wealthy elite, who felt that they were paying large sums of their vast wealth to help "the little people" have good schools and communities that worked. He changed laws like the Fairness Doctrine, in 1986, so that sycophants like Rush Limbaugh could appear on the public airwaves (with heavy corporate funding) to help convince the "average person" that taxes were bad and government was bad.

Reagan stopped enforcing the Sherman Antitrust Act, which since 1881 had held at bay the aggregation of corporate power, and the media began forming huge monopolies that were then used to reinforce on national TV and radio the perspectives of commentators like Limbaugh. Increasingly, across America two-, three-, and four-newspaper towns became one-newspaper towns, as the era of mergers and acquisitions swept the nation. Labor pages vanished from these new multistate, chain-owned newspapers and were replaced exclusively by "business sections." Labor almost entirely vanished from the American press.

An entire generation has been indoctrinated in this smaller-is-better view to the point where polls showed that when Bill Clinton said "smaller government," people reacted positively. Clinton signed the Telecommunications Act of 1996, the North American Free Trade Agreement (NAFTA), and the General Agreement on Tariffs and Trade (GATT), further reducing the power of We the People to regulate business and the media. The result was another explosion of mergers and the near total takeover of the American media and the American workplace by multinational corporations that have little or no allegiance to the USA or the concept of democracy. Today the bottom line rules and workers be damned.

But the cracks are now showing. In 2005 we found out just what happens when you follow Grover Norquist's advice and wash government down the drain. When Hurricane Katrina hit, more than a thousand people drowned in the basin of New Orleans. Our nation failed in its response because for most of the past twenty-five years cons who don't believe in governance have been systematically dismantling every aspect of our government except that part they can use to punish us or spy on us.

Here's the con game these pundits are playing: "smaller government" doesn't mean fewer taxes for you and me. It doesn't mean fewer politicians. It means government of, by, and for corporations and inherited wealth rather than of, by, and for We the People.

The cons' mantra is "Let the markets decide." But there is no "market" independent of government, so what they are really saying is "Let's make government work to help corporations instead of people. Let's provide all the services corporations need and then make the people foot the bill. Let's let corporations decide how much to pay for labor and when, where, and how to trade."

Thus "con government" is not "smaller government." Under George W. Bush, for example, inflation-adjusted government spending is as high as it was during World War II, at almost $20,000 per person per year.[1]

What the cons don't say is that the reason they want a smaller government is because they can then make an enormous amount of money when they privatize formerly governmental functions. They want a power vacuum so that corporations and the rich can step in and profit from things that used to be nonprofit.

Privatizing Social Security will bring a windfall to Wall Street. Our private health-care system has produced a huge crop of multimillionaires and multibillionaires like Bill Frist and his brother and father. One in twenty Americans is now getting tap water from a non-U.S. private corporation that is extracting profits from local American communities and taking those profits overseas. Large swaths of America's electrical infrastructure have been privatized *and* deregulated, leading to rate manipulation, brownouts in California, and huge profits for utility corporations. CEOs are looking forward to buying more Gulfstreams and nicer yachts, while America's middle class is paying more and more for basic and necessary services.

Making government smaller is a nice-sounding phrase in this post-Reagan world, but those who promote it are really pulling what Bernie Sanders[2] calls a "reverse Robin Hood." It's cover for a system that takes from the poor and gives to the rich.

In his budget proposal for 2007, Bush called for spending that will benefit the biggest U.S. corporations, including money for defense, drugs (under the new Medicare drug benefit), coal mining, and ethanol (that's corporate agriculture to you and me).[3] To pay for this corporate largess, Bush proposed cutting programs for the poorest among us, including the Commodity Supplemental Food Program, which provides food to low-income mothers with children. And he proposed further cutting programs that directly affect the middle class, including Medicare, education spending (including funding for arts education, parent resource centers, and education technology grants), and spending on the environment (including a program designed to update aging sewer systems and a $300 million cut to the Environmental Protection Agency).[4]

"Smaller government," it turns out, is not actually smaller government but different government. It's government for the rich instead of government for the rest of us. It's a departure from democracy and a shift toward the old hierarchical systems of kings and kingdoms, with the new kings being named Trump and Cheney and Bechtel and the new kingdoms being their corporations.

GOVERNING FOR PROFIT

In the corporatocracy, politicians are paid by economic interests rather than by We the People. Instead of fighting against this system, Reagan suggested that the problem was not the corporatocracy and its lobbyists but the existence of politicians and government. Reagan was the first American president to actually preach that his own job was a bad thing. His speechwriters once wrote for him: "Politics is supposed to be the second-oldest profession. I have come to realize that it bears a very close resemblance to the first."

The Jack Abramoff scandal of 2006 and the pervasive evidence that so many of our elected officials have been willing to trade their votes for cash demonstrates that politicians often act as if Reagan was right. But that's not the way it has to be.

Men like Thomas Jefferson (D), Abraham Lincoln (R), Theodore Roosevelt (R), and Franklin Roosevelt (D) were drawn to politics out of a sense of idealism, not a desire to advance their own interests. There really was a time when politicians chose politics because they wanted to represent the will of the people.

It seems that today's cons can't imagine anybody wanting to devote his or her life to the service of the nation. The highest calling in their minds is to make a profit.

Ronald Reagan certainly couldn't imagine why anyone would want to be in government. He said: "The best minds are not in government. If any were, business would hire them away."

This mind-set—that the only purpose for service in government is to set up the interests of business—may account for why not a single military-eligible member of the Bush or Cheney family enlisted in their parents' "noble cause," whereas all four sons of Franklin Roosevelt joined and each was decorated—on merit—for bravery in the deadly conflict of World War II. There are, after all, no reasons in the cons' worldview for government service other than self-enrichment.

The cons say they want smaller government—small enough to "drown in a bathtub"—but what they mean is that they want to provide government services only to business on the theory that what is good for business will eventually trickle down far enough to be good for the rest of us. And they admit that they expect to benefit very nicely themselves from aiding their superrich pals.

The cons don't really care about the "free" market. They care about taking care of their own. In fact, the cons are more than willing to toss their smaller-is-better mantra right out the window and grow government if it increases their profits and helps them stay in power.

GOVERNMENT FOR MY SIDE
AND NOT FOR YOURS

The cons aren't stupid. They know that government makes a real difference in people's lives. Look at the difference in the response to Hurricane Katrina in 2005 versus Hurricane Charley, which hit Jeb Bush's state a year earlier, just months before the 2004 elections.

Damage estimates from Katrina are well over $100 billion, with more than $34 billion in insured losses, according to the National Climatic Update Center.[5] This is four times more than the combined damage done by Hurricanes Charley, Frances, Ivan, and Jeanne in Florida last year, which came to almost $21 billion combined.[6]

We still don't know how many people died from Katrina, and we may never know. More than 1,300 bodies have been found, but more than two thousand people are considered "missing persons," who may have died in the hurricane and whose bodies may never be found.[7] By contrast Hurricane Charley caused the deaths of only eleven people.

But with Hurricane Charley, in Jeb Bush's red state, in the year of a presidential election, the response of the Federal Emergency Management Agency (FEMA) was considerably different than for blue-state Louisiana a year later. The day before Hurricane Charley hit, FEMA had mobilized 100 trucks of water, 900,000 Meals Ready to Eat (MREs), more than 7,000 cases of food, and tens of thousands of tarps. Disaster medical assistance teams, urban search-and-rescue teams, and FEMA officials were already in place; and 4,100 troops were called up and waiting to aid flood victims and assist in the distribution of supplies. In short, the government did exactly what it was supposed to do. The federal government was mailing checks to hurricane victims within a week of Charley's passing—including "victims" as far as 500 miles from the damage area.[8]

But when Katrina hit—with no election looming and with death stalking a Democratic state with a Democratic governor unrelated to the president—the Reagan philosophy held ascendant. George W. Bush's call to Americans in response to Hurricane Katrina? "Send cash to the Red Cross." While people were drowning, Bush traveled to Arizona to cut a birthday cake with John McCain and play golf; he then went to California, where he played guitar with a country singer at a fundraiser. It wasn't until three of his top aides drew straws to determine who would give him the bad news that people were dying—four days after the hurricane struck—that he saw a three-hour video they compiled of news reports over the past week and realized he needed to go into quick-PR mode and fly to Louisiana.

Vice President Dick Cheney stayed on vacation in Wyoming while thousands died in New Orleans; his former (and perhaps future) company, Halliburton, was busy, however, obtaining a multimillion-dollar contract to profit from Hurricane Katrina's cleanup.

Instead of preparing in advance, FEMA head Michael Brown waited until five hours after Katrina made landfall to finally ask his boss, Michael Chertoff, secretary of the Department of Homeland Security, for authorization for a thousand FEMA staff, active and reserves, to go into the flooded areas—and then suggested they be given two days to respond.[9] Chertoff, in turn, waited thirty-six hours to declare Katrina an "incident of national significance," which was necessary to trigger federal assistance.

Governor of Louisiana Kathleen Blanco asked FEMA if the mayor of New Orleans, Ray Nagin, should mobilize school and city buses to transport people out of the city; she was told by federal officials that he should not use them but instead wait for FEMA buses to arrive. The buses never came—the FEMA director and the Homeland Security director and the president and the vice president had more important business to attend to.

We all saw what happened next: thousands of people trapped in a flooded city with no food, no fuel, and no way out. No tents, trailers, or other temporary shelters were made ready before Katrina struck, leaving those whose homes had been destroyed to gather in the Superdome for days on end.

The aftermath hasn't been much better. Though Congress has appropriated more than $85 million, the Republican Party itself noted that the Bush administration had misspent much of it. As I write this, New Orleans is still a mess and they're still finding bodies.

When it benefited one of their own, the cons sure knew how to make use of government in Florida. Louisiana, however, was another matter.

American democracy was not designed as a government of, by, and for special interests. It is a government of, by, and for We the People. And it's time We the People took it back.

GOVERNING REQUIRES GOVERNMENT

A listener to my radio program called in and pointed out: "You can't govern if you don't believe in government."

The conservatives who are now in the driver's seat are steering us away from government. But when you diminish the role of government, you aren't left with a "free" market. You're left with feudalism.

When George W. Bush and his cronies say that they want to make government smaller, they are making explicit their undeclared war on the middle class. We can't expect the cons to have a change of heart: that occurs only in fiction. If we want to preserve a middle class in America—and the democracy that the middle class alone can maintain—we must take our government back.

CHAPTER 2

How We the People Create the Middle Class

On October 19, 2003, the *New York Times* ran an article about Levi Strauss, the maker of all-American denim jeans.[1] After January 2004, Levi's jeans stopped being made in America. No more American Levi's. That's like saying America doesn't make apple pie anymore.

Does outsourcing Levi's matter? It matters to Mrs. Flores, who was profiled in the *Times* article. Mrs. Flores worked for Levi's for twenty-four years and was a member of her local union. She was making $18 per hour, got four weeks' paid vacation, and had full family medical and dental benefits for a payment of just $24 per week. Mrs. Flores was in the middle class.

But Mrs. Flores knows she won't be middle class for long if conservatives get their way. "Where am I going to get a job like this?" she asked in the article. After NAFTA and the World Trade Organization (WTO)—the conservative "free" trade policies—took effect in 1994–1995, this country lost 785,000 apparel jobs.

What's happening to people like Mrs. Flores—to the middle class—is not an unforeseen consequence of "free" trade. The policies the cons advocate have historically led nations to become societies in which one is either aristocratic or impoverished. Follow the cons' economics, and very rich people will become so rich and powerful they will create dynastic empires (like the Bushes) while huge numbers of formerly middle-class people become destitute—and there's little in between.

If we want to keep a healthy middle class and the strong democracy it will maintain, we can't just stand idly by while the cons do their damage. If a nation wants a middle class, it must define it, desire it, and work to both create it and keep it.

A middle class is the creation of government participation in the marketplace, balancing out the anti-democratic power of the economic kingdoms we call corporations.

We create a middle class in three ways:

- ▶ By creating and regulating the rules of the game of business

- ▶ By protecting jobs inside the country with rational tariffs and trade policies

- ▶ By providing—to all—a healthy social safety net and the means for social mobility, such as a free public education—all the way through college

Government of, by, and for the people requires a return to classical economic policies that put We the People in the driver's seat. We know that these policies work because we've tried them before and they created one of the strongest middle classes the world has ever seen. They're in use today in countries from Brazil to Sweden. When the cons tried imposing their utopian free-trade, flat-tax, trickle-down theories on Iraq, it led to a total meltdown. Con economics have never produced democracy or a middle class anywhere. And in America all they've done over the years since Reagan first instituted them is to crush a large sector of the middle class and put our democracy up for sale to the highest bidder.

AMERICA'S FIRST MIDDLE CLASS

The United States has had two great periods of what we today call a middle class. The first was from the 1700s to the mid-1800s and was fueled by the transfer of land from Native Americans to settlers—a great deal for the settlers, who got the land virtually for free, and a raw deal for the Native Americans. With cheap land as their capital, ordinary Americans could become the "citizen farmers" whom Alexis de Tocqueville idealized in his 1834 masterpiece *Democracy in America*—average people, living in relative self-sufficiency, neither rich nor poor but fully literate and well informed about politics and international affairs.

That land-based middle class lasted from roughly the founding of this nation through the Civil War, when "free land" was becoming scarce and the industrial revolution was drawing workers into the cities in search of work. As big business grew in the 1880s after the Civil War, the farm-based middle class collapsed, in large part because the early progenitors of companies like today's Cargill and Archer Daniels Midland Company gained control of the sale and the distribution of farm produce. Middle-class farmers rose up, creating the Grange Movement as part of their own way of competing with the big-agriculture companies. But the country was moving from an agricultural base to an industrial one, which compounded the farmers' loss of power.

As industry grew, the nation entered a period sometimes referred to as the Robber Baron Era or the Gilded Age. Wealthy capitalists obtained monopolies over new technology and the resources it required—railroads, steelworks, oil—and amassed huge amounts of wealth. That wealth did not reach their workers, however.

By the start of the twentieth century, the average income of working Americans was less than $10,000 per year in today's dollars. Americans did not sit still. We fought back through the Progressive and Populist movements, gaining significant economic and political reforms. Their first step was to limit the size of corporations to limit their power—hence the Sherman Antitrust Act of 1881. (It's still law but is unenforced for all practical purposes since Reagan ordered its enforcement scaled back. Jimmy

Carter was the last president to use it meaningfully, to break up the AT&T monopoly.)

Step two was to take Theodore Roosevelt's advice: "We must drive the special interests out of politics. The citizens of the United States must effectively control the mighty commercial forces which they have themselves called into being. There can be no effective control of corporations while their political activity remains." Progressives pushed hard, and in 1907 a law was passed (which is still on the books), making it illegal for corporations to give money to politicians. It needs to be expanded.

Other parts of the progressive agenda were political rather than purely economic in nature. They included legislating the direct election of U.S. senators who previously had been appointed by political machines in the states. Progressives at the turn of the century also hoped that if women could get the vote, they would help break up the old boy club of big business. (These goals were achieved in 1913 and 1920.) Even in the face of corporate violence that often escalated to murder, Americans struggled to bring together the budding union movement.

Once an aristocracy is in place, however, it is hard to dislodge. Even though American citizens were very politically active during this time, by and large the vast majority had little say in their own economic destiny. The Gilded Age saw a very Dickensian America—a small group of very wealthy businessmen and landowners and a very large class of desperately poor workers.

THE NEW DEAL

The Great Depression was the spark that lit the beginnings of America's second era of a middle class. By 1929, after a series of massive tax cuts for the wealthy by two successive Republican presidents, the chasm between the wealth of the "investor class" and that of the working class in the United States was greater than it had ever been. (It again reached these dimensions—for only the second time in U.S. history—in the autumn of 2005.) The result was the October 1929 stock market crash and the Great Depression that followed.

Although Herbert Hoover ran his 1932 presidential campaign on the slogan *Prosperity Is Just Around the Corner,* by that time few Americans were buying his idea of more tax cuts for millionaires. They also weren't happy with an extremist Supreme Court that had recently struck down minimum wage and other worker protection laws as unconstitutional. They voted in massive numbers for Franklin D. Roosevelt, who campaigned relentlessly on a platform of government involvement in the marketplace to restore both democracy and the middle class.

It took the leadership of President Roosevelt in the 1930s for the government to again take a hand in creating a middle class, this time via industrialized labor instead of land. FDR implemented the two necessary economic ingredients—a classical economic model and a government-spending stimulus—thereby almost single-handedly creating the modern middle class.

FDR made sure that We the People had money in our pockets through progressive taxation, Social Security, fair labor laws, the regulation of business, and the vigorous enforcement of antitrust laws. In 1935 he pushed through the Fair Labor Standards Act, which set a minimum wage, and the National Labor Relations Act (Wagner Act), which protected workers' right to create a democratic institution—a union that elected its own leadership—in the feudal kingdoms of America's workplaces. People like Mrs. Flores, sewing Levi's, were for the first time able to negotiate a living wage.

During World War II, FDR passed a progressive income tax that barely touched the working class and the middle class but took up to 90 percent of the income *after* a person earned what would be more than $2 million in today's dollars.[2] That rate remained high under FDR, Truman, Eisenhower, Kennedy, Nixon, Johnson, and Carter. America's debt was relatively small, and progressive taxation kept money in the pockets of the people most likely to spend it and stimulate consumer demand.

Some say that World War II was the stimulus out of the Depression, and it was an economic stimulus from which many, like the Bush family businesses, benefited (until Prescott Bush lost one of his companies for doing business with Hitler while we were at war); but spending money on weapons doesn't stimulate an economy the way building roads, bridges, houses, or domestic consumer industries, which "keep on giving," does. The real events of the 1930s and 1940s that set the stage for a second American middle class were primarily the social spending programs that FDR created and integrated with unionization, antitrust laws, and the expansion of citizen participation in our democracy that inevitably occurs when a middle class grows.

In a time of crisis, instead of giving tax cuts to billionaires, FDR went directly to the working class to stimulate the economy. The Civilian Conservation Corps hired young men ages eighteen to twenty-five to plant trees, create animal sanctuaries, fight pollution, and maintain the national forests. The Public Works Administration paid skilled construction workers to build infrastructure, including the Triborough Bridge in New York City. The Works Progress Administration (later the Works Projects Administration, or WPA) put thousands more to work improving our country, paying skilled craftsmen and artists to put on plays, create murals, build buildings, and otherwise improve the commons. Each of these programs paid a living wage, providing a direct stimulus to the economy.

FDR made sure that Americans would be able to enjoy the fruits of their labor by establishing Social Security. A government-run insurance program, Social Security continues to provide money for the disabled while ensuring that all working Americans have some savings for retirement.

In addition to creating a strong economy, FDR acted to control the game of business. He set up the Federal Deposit Insurance Corporation (FDIC) to ensure that people would be able to keep the money they saved in banks. He imposed regulations on stock sales, protecting middle-class people who invested their savings in the stock market. He moved against monopolies through the Public Utility Holding Company Act of 1935, which broke up large electrical conglomerates, and he fought for an expansion of existing antitrust legislation.

Along with fighting for the rights of We the People in the present, Roosevelt looked to the future. He furthered the cause of public education through the GI Bill, which sent millions of young men and women to college and technical schools in the late 1940s and early 1950s. Although it was never carefully measured, some historians suggest that well over half of the GI Bill college graduates in the 1950s were the first in their families to graduate from college. Not only did this provide America with a huge competitive edge in an educated workforce but it also represented the first and largest shift in American history of people from the ranks of the working poor into the ranks of the working middle class. Not until Lyndon Baines Johnson declared a War on Poverty in the 1960s, cutting poverty in half in its first four years, would a program so effectively provide for social mobility.

Roosevelt's programs worked. His economic stimulus programs put money in the pockets of the people, and their purchases created consumer demand, which led entrepreneurs to start businesses to meet that demand, which meant they had to hire workers, who were well paid because 35 percent of America was unionized. Those well-paid workers bought more goods, creating more demand, and America became the world's strongest economy through most of the twentieth century. The New Deal ushered in what has been called the Golden Age of the middle class, from 1940 to 1980.

The basic philosophy of the New Deal was a fusion of the thinking of Thomas Paine and Thomas Jefferson—a platform of progressive economics and personal freedom combined with the empowerment of the average person. Roosevelt's message to business was simple: you're welcome to make money in America—in fact, we *want* you to—but you must understand that you are making money within our society, using the superstructure and the substructure of our democracy, and therefore you are answerable to our democracy. The economy exists to serve the members of our democracy, not the other way around. If you want to play the game of business, you're welcome to do so according to our new rules, which protect workers and consumers, provide for the creation of a middle class, and keep the government democratic.

In a very real way, Franklin Roosevelt saved capitalism from itself.

Now the cons are working as hard and as fast as they can to take Roosevelt's programs apart. "Roosevelt is dead!" Rush Limbaugh declared. "His programs live on, but we're in the process of doing something about that as well."

We can push back against the cons and revitalize the American middle class by resetting the rules of the game of business, by implementing economic stimulus programs and restoring progressive taxation, and by supporting national health care and free public education that extends all the way through college.

SETTING THE RULES OF BUSINESS

The cons' willingness to make sure the rest of us stay poor and unhappy is well documented. On the front page of the *Wall Street Journal* on January 27, 1997, the newspaper that represents the voice of what it calls the "investor class" pointed out how con and former Federal Reserve Board chairman Alan Greenspan saw one of his main responsibilities to be maintaining a high-enough level of worker insecurity that employees wouldn't demand pay raises and benefit increases:

> Workers' fear of losing their jobs restrains them from seeking the pay raises that usually crop up when employers have trouble finding people to hire.
>
> Even if the economy didn't slow down as he expected, he [Alan Greenspan] told fed colleagues last summer, he saw little danger of a sudden upturn in wages and prices.
>
> "Because workers are more worried about their own job security and their marketability if forced to change jobs, they are apparently accepting smaller increases in their compensation at any given level of labor-market tightness," Mr. Greenspan told Congress at that time.[3]

The Founders of this nation are spinning in their graves.

Thomas Jefferson, the founder of the Democratic Party, did not want business to profit at the expense of We the People. The democratic government he was creating was designed to function for the benefit of the people and not the benefit of business. He wrote in 1816 in a letter to Samuel Kercheval:

> Those seeking profits, were they given total freedom, would not be the ones to trust to keep government pure and our rights secure. Indeed, it has always been those seeking wealth who were the source of corruption in government. No other depositories of power have ever yet been found, which did not end in converting to their own profit the earnings of those committed to their charge.

It is a founding principle of the United States of America that government has both the right and the responsibility to set the rules of business. Jefferson, in an 1816 letter to William H. Crawford, wrote, "Every society has a right to fix the fundamental principles of association." If you want to create a business that deals with the public, you have to abide by the public's rules.

Markets are a creation of government, just as corporations exist only by authorization of government. Governments set the rules of the market. And because our government is of, by, and for We the People, those rules have historically been set to maximize the public good resulting from people's doing business.

Government can set the rules of the game of business in such a way that working people must receive a living wage, that labor has the power to organize into unions just as capital can organize into corporations, and that domestic industries can be protected from overseas competition. When these rules are combined with a democratic form of government, a strong middle class will emerge.

When government gives up this rule-making function, the middle class vanishes and we return to the cons' Dickens-era form of economics, where the rich get richer and the working poor are kept in a constant state of fear and anxiety so the cost of their labor will always be cheap. And democracy dies.

Jefferson knew that some people would prefer that government not play the role of referee. He knew that free marketeers (yes, they existed back then) would not want to accept rules designed to protect labor or the commons or the public good. Too bad, he said. We the People write the rules of business to eliminate "dangers which the society chooses to avoid." If corporations don't like the rules, we must "say to all [such] individuals, that if they contemplate pursuits beyond the limits of these principles, . . . they must go somewhere else for their exercise; that we want no citizens, and still less ephemeral and pseudo-citizens [like corporations], on such terms."

Jefferson told Kercheval:

> I am not among those who fear the people. They, and not the rich, are our dependence for continued freedom. . . . We must make our election between economy and liberty, or profusion and servitude. . . . [Otherwise], as the people of England are, our people, like them, must come to labor sixteen hours in the twenty-four, . . . and the sixteenth being insufficient to afford us

bread, we must live, as they now do, on oatmeal and potatoes; have no time to think, no means of calling the mismanagers to account; but be glad to obtain subsistence by hiring ourselves to rivet their chains on the necks of our fellow sufferers.

If the United States allowed a totally "free" market where corporations reigned supreme, according to Jefferson, America would become just like the oppressive governments of old, transformed

until the bulk of the society is reduced to be mere automatons of misery, to have no sensibilities left but for sinning and suffering. Then begins, indeed, the *bellum omnium in omnia* [the war of all with all], which some philosophers observing to be so general in this world, have mistaken it for the natural, instead of the abusive state of man.

As Jefferson realized, with no government "interference" by setting the rules of the game of business, there will be no middle class. And without a middle class, democracy won't survive.

RETURNING TO CLASSICAL ECONOMICS

Ronald Reagan's favorite punch line was: "I've always felt the nine most terrifying words in the English language are 'I'm from the government and I'm here to help.'"

Sure, it's easy to laugh along and think that government is bad—until you need government. Until you've been taken advantage of and want to use the government court system, or you get old and sick and need Medicare, or your house catches fire and you'd like your local fire department to come by and put it out.

Reagan often used to say that the government is stealing your money. The cons love that mantra: "It's your money."

Nobody *likes* to pay taxes. And nearly three decades of deceitful PR convincing Americans that there's no need to invest in our nation—and, thus, no need to pay for it with taxes—has left us with an electorate that so hates the word *tax* that cons can use it to turn voters against almost anyone advocating any government program. If you're a politician and someone calls you a "tax-and-spend liberal," that generally means "good-bye to your votes." The cons exploit this with the "It's your money" lie. "It's *your* money, and the liberals want it!" shout cons on the radio. They're talking about taxes, of course. But are our tax dollars really "our" money?

If I walk into a 7-Eleven store with a dollar in my pocket and say, "Gee, I'd really like that Hershey bar," and if I tear it open and take a bite out of it, that Hershey bar now belongs to me. And that dollar belongs to 7-Eleven, *even though it's still in my pocket.* It's pretty simple. As soon as I used the candy bar, I'd entered into an agreement to pay for it. It's a form of a contract even though I've never signed anything with a convenience store in my life. It's not my money anymore, even though it's still in my pocket, once I take possession of the candy bar.

We make an agreement by staying in this country that we will live by its rules.

I get up in the morning and the lights come on because my government is regulating the local utility for both safety and reliability. (FDR had to *force* electric utilities to serve many communities—thus the Rural Electrification Administration.) I open the tap to brush my teeth, and the water is pure because my government has purified it and delivered it to me from miles away in a safe fashion. The toothpaste I use isn't poisonous because the government passed laws that make it possible for aggrieved consumers to sue if they're harmed. Its ingredients are listed because the government requires it.

When I drive to work, the streets are paved by my government, and the streetlights work because my government planned them right and keeps them in good working order. The radio station where I broadcast from can do business because my government provides a stable currency and a framework of contract laws that allow a corporation to exist and function. The food I eat for lunch at a nearby restaurant is safe both because it was inspected at its source by the U.S. Department of Agriculture and because the local government checks our restaurants for sanitary conditions. I can eat without worrying that bandits are going to run into the restaurant and demand everybody's wallet because the police are on the job. And I can go about my day without worrying that we'll be bombed by invaders from another country because the State Department and the U.S. Army both negotiate and protect our nation. With a little bit of thought, you can add dozens of other things to this list—all provided with taxpayer dollars.

Living in this society and using these services is like picking up and biting into the Hershey bar at the 7-Eleven: I've agreed to pay for them because I live here and I use them. The form of my agreement is called taxes. Therefore the money from my paycheck that goes to pay my taxes is *not* my money. It's the money I owe to cover the cost associated with the things I use each and every day. To suggest that it's "my" money is to spit in the face of our Founders—to suggest that somehow each of us is above and separate from the social contract we've all agreed to by living in this great nation.

When the cons say, "It's your money," what they really mean is that they don't believe in the social contract. They don't believe in paying for the services we use every day or in taking care of the poor and the sick and the elderly who can't take care of themselves. They are anti-American, anti-democracy, anti-Christian (and anti-Jewish and anti–every other major religion) zealots. They are a danger to our democracy and our country.

Progressive taxation has a long history. Jefferson advocated for progressive taxation in his letters to James Madison back in 1784 and 1785: "Another means of silently lessening the inequality of property," Jefferson wrote, "is to exempt all from taxation below a certain point, and to tax the higher portions of property in geometrical progression as they rise." In short, Jefferson said, "Taxes should be proportioned to what may be annually spared by the individual."

But the cons—who since the days when John Adams called working people "the rabble"—fought back. A true middle class represented a threat to America's aristocrats and pseudo-aristocrats because a middle class will always create a democracy. The cons would have to give up some of their power, and some of the higher end of their wealth might even be "redistributed"—horror of horrors—for schools, parks, libraries, and other things that support a healthy middle-class society (but not necessarily the rich, who live in a parallel, but separate, world).

When today's cons make *tax* a dirty word, they are really saying they don't care if the middle class gets screwed. As president, Reagan cut the top tax rate for billionaires from 70 percent to 28 percent while effectively raising taxes on working people via the payroll tax; he added insult to injury by allowing inflation to increase a whole range of taxes (sales tax, property tax, vehicle license fees, and so on) on working people. Following in that tradition, the Bush Jr. administration gave, in its first four years, tax cuts totaling almost half a trillion dollars to the best-off 1 percent of Americans.[4]

Even as taxes on the rich go down, they've gone up on the middle class (in part *because* they've gone down for the rich and *somebody* has to pay the cost of all the commons we use). If you made $75,000 in 2001, you saw only $350 in tax cuts from the federal government. In 2005, 80 percent of Americans got only 32 percent of the total tax-cut pie. That means the wealthiest 20 percent of Americans got 68 percent of the money the government was "giving back to the people." Unless you were making more than $218,000 a year in 2005, you got screwed by Bush's tax cuts.[5]

It's all part of the cons' undeclared war on the middle class.

FREE PUBLIC EDUCATION

A study in 2003 by a researcher at Yale University revealed that more than 50 percent of first-year college students couldn't produce papers free of grammatical errors—in simple language, they can't write. Eighty percent of graduating high school seniors say they will never again voluntarily read another book. Only one-third of U.S. students are proficient readers; two-thirds lack sufficient reading ability to comprehend novels, textbooks, this book, and other forms of "complicated writing."

Democracy requires an educated middle class for its survival. At its most simple level, alone among political systems, democracy requires citizens to vote for the country's leaders and policies. If you can't read the ballot, if you don't know enough math to understand the economic argument a politician is making, if you don't know the history of the country and our laws, how can you decide how to vote?

Alexis de Tocqueville came to America in 1834 to figure out how Americans were making democracy work. Along the way he met with a pig farmer, just a simple country bumpkin by de Tocqueville's reasoning, and asked him about international politics. And this farmer went into an insightful, knowledgeable rant about French politics. De Tocqueville's conclusion was that a well-educated populace was essential to democracy—and that, unlike France in that era, we had one here.

Jefferson agreed. He advocated a national program of free education up to and including university. In an 1824 letter, he explained why: "This degree of [free] education would . . . give us a body of yeomanry, too, of substantial information, well prepared to become a firm and steady support to the government."

True to his word, Jefferson started the University of Virginia to provide free higher education to the yeomanry, which is what the middle class was called back in the 1700s. The state university system grew slowly over the years and really picked up under FDR.

But that didn't last long.

Governor Ronald Reagan ended free enrollment at the last state university system to offer it, the University of California, in 1966. Today government funding for higher education is at minimal levels, particularly compared with Europe and Japan, where in most cases university educations are free or nearly free. Although there are still some educational benefits for GIs, they're hard to accumulate, track, and qualify for (and must be paid for in most cases). Under George W. Bush, even the student loan program has been cut significantly, and eligibility for grants to low-income students—called Pell Grants—has decreased dramatically; in 2004 alone, for example, Bush cut eighty thousand students off the eligibility list for Pell Grants.

Now the Bush administration wants to privatize K–12 education, as well. Bush advocates replacing free public education with "tuition vouchers" good at private schools, including parochial schools and for-profit schools. His No Child Left Behind Act set up thirty-seven ways public schools could fail. A failing school is sanctioned under the act with a loss of funds—so that schools that need the most help get the least. By September 2004, 36 percent of California's schools had already been put on that list.[6] Instead of being a program to improve public education, No Child Left Behind was designed to kill the public school system.

AMERICA'S FUTURE

Every generation, it is often said, must relearn the lessons of history. This generation is getting a crash course.

Education for the few rather than the many, tax breaks for the rich but higher taxes for the middle class, a market where the corporations make all the rules—the last time America looked like this was during the Gilded Age, the era of the robber barons.

There's nothing wrong with business making money. I've owned seven businesses, and I'm proud to say that I made money at all but one of them. But there is something wrong when hard-working people like Mrs. Flores can't get a full-time job that pays a living wage. There's something wrong when people with college educations can't earn enough money to buy a house. There's something wrong when it's nearly impossible to pay for a college education at all. There's something wrong when almost everyone you know feels screwed.

CHAPTER 3

The Rise of the Corporatocracy

Walking through a park on a sunny summer day in Portland, Oregon, I stumbled across a stunning example of what has happened to the middle class in the cons' America.

Thirty or more people were sitting on blankets and lawn chairs under a big oak tree in a semicircle around a middle-aged, suit-wearing woman with a flip chart. Those in the circle wore mostly casual clothes, and the average age seemed to be midforties, although there were a few as young as midtwenties and a few who looked to be in their sixties. Two men in the group—both in their fifties, by appearance—had gone to the trouble of dressing in business suits, although they looked painfully uncomfortable sitting on their lawn chairs in the open park.

As I walked by, I heard the woman extolling the virtues of "cheerfulness" and rhetorically asking her students, "Would *you* want to hire you?"

Welcome to the world of those who have fallen out of America's white-collar middle class and are tapping their IRAs, 401(k)s, and overextended credit cards to pay for workshops like this one to figure out how they can get decent-paying jobs to replace the ones they've lost.

The seminar I heard might help a few of these people—I hope it did—but it won't help America get back on track. The middle class doesn't need a pep talk. Americans are the most dedicated and productive workers in the world. Judging from their appearance, most of the folks in that circle had worked hard and done their best all their lives—and been screwed anyway.

THE NEW FEUDAL LORDS: THE CORPORATOCRACY

How could the American middle class—the greatest middle class in the world—be in so much trouble?

Consider the biggest pocketbook pincher: health care. Many Americans are falling out of the middle class today because they can't afford health insurance. One bad accident, one serious illness, one really big hospital bill, and that's it—they can't pay the bills, so they lose their car and their home and tumble right out of the middle class.

Back in my dad's day, that wouldn't have happened. Most working people got health care through their employers. The big health-care insurers—Blue Cross and Blue Shield—were nonprofits, which meant that they just passed on the actual cost of health insurance to employers. The government implemented Medicare and Medicaid in the 1960s to take care of all the folks who weren't insured. Although the system worked imperfectly, overall it was pretty decent.

But then Reagan deregulated hospitals and much of the rest of the health-care industry (along with trucking, travel, and a dozen other industries). Within a decade the system had fallen apart for all but the wealthiest Americans. Hospitals, which had been mainly nonprofit, became for-profit and started charging higher rates. Drug companies realized they could raise prices as high as they wanted because they had bought out their competitors in Reagan's merger-and-acquisition mania and no longer have government looking over their shoulders. Pharmaceutical companies are now the most profitable business in the United States.[1] Insurance companies got into the act too, going from nonprofit to for-profit. Every player in the system started looking to health care to make a buck. The result was double-digit health-care inflation rates by 2001.[2]

Government tried a number of times to rein in these costs, with little success.[3] Bill Clinton proposed a modest public/private national health-care plan, but such a plan could trim corporate profits, and the cons fought back with a level of deceit and ferocity not seen since the battles against Franklin Roosevelt in the 1930s.

The cons responded to Clinton's plan by asking Americans, over and over again, "Do you want government bureaucrats deciding which doctor you can see?"

As a yes-or-no question, the answer was pretty simple for most Americans: no. But, as is so often the case when the cons try to influence public opinion, the true issue wasn't honestly stated.

The real question was: Do you want government bureaucrats, answerable to elected officials and thus subject to the will of We the People, making decisions about your health care, *or would you rather have corporate bureaucrats, answerable only to their CEOs and working in a profit-driven environment, making decisions about your health care?*

The cons don't believe in We the People. They believe that our economy—and our society—would run better if a few elites at the top made decisions for the rest of us. They really do think we'd be better off if a few corporate CEOs ran health care. When the cons call for smaller government or for less regulation or for "free" markets, what they are really saying is: "Give control of the economy over to a handful of CEOs and let us run the country for you."

What they're really saying is that they don't believe in democracy and don't want a middle class.

DON'T BLAME THE AMERICAN MIDDLE CLASS

When the cons are confronted with the growing gap between the rich and the poor in America, they know exactly what to do: blame us.

That's what Ben Bernanke, the chairman of the Federal Reserve, told Congress in his first appearance before that body in February 2006. When Representative Barney Frank asked Bernanke about income inequality, Bernanke replied that the reason for that inequality is "the increased return to education." That's economists' language for saying, "Americans aren't well enough educated to take the many jobs that would be available to them if they knew more."

New York Times columnist Paul Krugman said in response, "That's a fundamental misreading of what's happening in American society."[4] While college graduates do make more, on average, than those without a BA, it's not true that there are jobs just waiting for Americans who educate themselves. According to Krugman, the "2006 Economic Report of the President" indicates that "the real earnings of college graduates actually fell more than 5 percent between 2000 and 2004." It's just not true that those who are better educated are much better off.

So who *is* better off? Well, between 1972 and 2001, the income of Americans at the 90th percentile of the income distribution—that is, college graduates, white-collar workers, and people at the higher end of the middle class—rose 34 percent, or about 1 percent per year. That's not really enough to keep up with inflation, so where did the money go? Krugman, quoting a Northwestern University research study,[5] tells us:

Income at the 99th percentile rose 87 percent.

Income at the 99.9th percentile rose 181 percent.

Income at the 99.99th percentile rose 497 percent.

If you are at the 99.9th percentile, you have an income of at least $1,672,726 per year. Those in the 99.99th percentile have an income well over $6 million. And those are the people who made the most money in America over the past two decades.

America's income inequality is not because Americans aren't smart enough. America has income inequality because a small elite group of corporate aristocrats have decided that they deserve to make more money than the rest of us. And they justify their greed and questionable business practices by saying that the market knows best.

One con, Michael Powell, said as much. In an NPR *Morning Edition* report on May 28, 2003, Rick Carr reported: "Current FCC Chair Michael Powell says he has faith the market will provide. What's more, he says, he'd rather have the market decide than government." Powell was reciting the cons' mantra. Misconstruing Adam Smith, who in 1776 warned about the dangers of the invisible hand in the marketplace trampling the rights and the needs of the people, the cons suggest that business always knows best.

In the cons' brave new world, corporations are more suited to governance than are the unpredictable rabble of the citizenry. Corporations should control politics, control the commons, control health care, control our airwaves, control the "free" market, and even control our schools.

Although corporations can't vote, the cons claim they should have human rights, like privacy from government inspections of their political activities and the free-speech right to lie to politicians and citizens in PR and advertising.

Although corporations don't need to breathe fresh air or drink pure water, the cons would hand over to them the power to self-regulate their poisonous emissions into our air and water.

Corporations and their CEOs are America's new feudal lords, and the lower-level cons are their obliging servants and mouthpieces. Instead of a landed aristocracy, we increasingly have a corporate aristocracy. Call it *corporatocracy.*

FEUDALIST TAKEOVER

America was not conceived of as a feudal state, *feudalism* being broadly defined as rule by the superrich. Our nation was created in large part in reaction *against* centuries of European feudalism. As Ralph Waldo Emerson said in his lecture titled "The Fortune of the Republic," delivered on December 1, 1863, "We began with freedom. America was opened after the feudal mischief was spent. No inquisitions here, no kings, no nobles, no dominant church."

The founding idea of America was that our country would not be ruled by a handful of very powerful, very rich men. America was founded as a country ruled by We the People, and for democracy to work there had to be a strong and broad-based middle class.

Even at our country's founding, there were some who couldn't quite shake the idea that aristocracy was the way to go. As Jefferson warned in an 1826 letter to William B. Giles, there were those even then who

> look to a single and splendid government of an aristocracy, founded on banking institutions, and moneyed incorporations under the guise and cloak of their favored branches of manu-factures, commerce and navigation, riding and ruling over the plundered ploughman and beggared yeomanry. This will be to them a next best blessing to the monarchy of their first aim, and perhaps the surest steppingstone to it.

The aristocracy Jefferson feared first rose during the Gilded Age in the 1880s, when just a few companies seized control of much of America, including many of our elected officials. The ma-jor form of transportation and communication in those days was the railroad—and the railroads were owned by the Vanderbilts. The major form of energy then as today was oil, monopolized by John D. Rockefeller's Standard Oil Trust. And the major form of trade was in manufactured goods, which required factories, which in turn required steel—monopolized by Andrew Carnegie and his Carnegie Steel Company. These monopolists required ways to retain their hold on their money, so they turned to financiers like Jay Gould and John Pierpont Morgan, who set up large trusts for them.

The Progressive Movement and then FDR beat back these monopolists with the Sherman Antitrust Act, the National Labor Relations Act (Wagner Act), and other laws that regulated the game of business. Then Ronald Reagan, George Bush Sr., Bill Clinton, and George Bush Jr. came along and turned back the clock. Reagan fought the labor laws, Bush Sr. pushed for fast-track trade authority for the president, Clinton finally took down trade protections, and Bush Jr. put corporate executives into the driver's seat on government legislation.

We've entered a new Robber Baron Era.

Today the major form of communication is by phone and the Internet, an area increasingly monopolized by the new AT&T (formerly SBC/Cingular/AT&T). The major form of energy—oil—is controlled by just a handful of companies. Today's economic driver is the computer; its software is monopolized by Microsoft, and its hardware is manufactured by a handful of oligarchs.

Today, as in the Gilded Age, the rich are richer than ever. Forbes crows that in 2005 the "rich got richer" as "the collective net worth of the United States' wealthiest climbed $125 billion, to $1.13 trillion."[6] That's greater than the gross domestic product of Spain or Canada. Bill Gates alone is worth $51 billion. Five Walton family members—the owners of Wal-Mart—made it into the top 10.

Meanwhile, the median household income fell for the fifth year in a row to $44,389 in 2004—down from $46,129 in 1999, adjusting for inflation.[7] In 1972 the median income for a person with a high school diploma was the equivalent of $42,630 in today's dollars. In 2002, the last year for which the National Center for Education Statistics compiled such numbers, a person with a high school diploma has a median income of $29,647.[8] As the rich got richer, the rest of us got poorer—particularly what used to be our middle class.

The hallmark of the corporatocracy is monopoly—fewer people holding more of the wealth, fewer companies owning more of the commons. The very competition that the cons claim to embrace is destroyed by the unrestrained growth of corporate interests. Big fish eat little fish, over and over, until there are no little fish left. Then they eat the middle-sized fish until they're gone, too.

Look at the thoroughfares of any American city and ask yourself how many of the businesses there are locally owned. Instead of cash circulating within a local economy, at midnight every night a button is pushed and the local money from all over America is vacuumed away to Little Rock or Chicago or New York.

And the corporate lords want more.

Not content with their hold over the private sector, they want to take over the public sector, too. When Jeb Bush cut a deal with Enron to privatize the Everglades, it diminished the power of the Florida government to protect a natural resource and enhanced the power and the profitability of Enron. Similarly, when politicians argue for harsher sentencing guidelines and also advocate more corporate-owned prisons, they're enhancing the power and the profits of one of America's fastest-growing and most profitable remaining domestic industries: privately owned prisons.

The cons look at the government's pollution controls and see regulations that get in the way of their profits. They look at single-payer health care and see a threat to the pharmaceutical industry's practice of price-gouging Americans. They look at Social Security and see an opportunity for more big bonuses for more Wall Street fat cats. In these and other areas, the government still holds the keys to the riches of the commons held in trust for us all—riches the corporations want to convert into profits no matter if it destroys America's middle class and kills off our democracy.

The cons confuse efficiency and cost. They suggest that big corporations can perform public services at a lower total cost than government can, while ignoring the corporate need to pad the bill with dividends to stockholders, inflated CEO salaries, corporate jets and headquarters, advertising, millions in campaign contributions, and cash set-asides for growth and expansion. They frame corporate ownership as the solution of the "free" market and talk about entrepreneurs and small businesses filling up the holes left when government lets go of public property.

But these are straw man arguments. When the cons say that government is the enemy, they disguise their real agenda. The government of the United States is *us*. It was designed to be a government of, by, and for We the People. It's not an enemy to be destroyed; it's a means by which we administer and preserve the commons that we collectively own. When the cons try to "drown government in a bathtub," what they are really doing is replacing democracy with corporate rule, a feudal state controlled exclusively by the largest of the corporations. They are calling for nothing less than the destruction of the middle class—and thus democracy—in the United States of America.

NOBLES NEED NOT PAY TAXES

A cornerstone of the cons' movement to consolidate power in the hands of a wealthy corporate elite is the campaign to end corporate income taxes altogether—and leave the rest of us to pick up the entire tab for corporate use of our institutions and corporate despoliation of our commons.

Corporations are taxed because they use public services; they are therefore expected to help pay for them—sort of like the example in chapter 2 of the Hershey bar in the 7-Eleven store.

Corporations make use of a workforce educated in public schools that are paid for with tax dollars. They use roads and highways paid for with tax dollars. They use water, sewer, power, and communications rights of way paid for and maintained with taxes. They demand the same protection from fire and police departments as everybody else, and they enjoy the benefits of national sovereignty and the stability provided by the military and institutions like the United Nations and the North Atlantic Treaty Organization (NATO), the same as all residents of democratic nations.

In fact, corporations are *heavier* users of taxpayer-provided services and institutions than are average citizens. Taxes pay for our court systems, which are most heavily used by corporations to enforce contracts. Taxes pay for our Treasury Department and other government institutions that maintain a stable currency essential to corporate activity. Taxes pay for our regulation of corporate activity, from ensuring safety in the workplace and a pure food and drug supply to limiting toxic emissions in our air and water.

Under George W. Bush, the burden of cleaning up toxic wastes produced by corporate activity has largely shifted from the original polluter-funded Superfund and other programs to taxpayer-funded cleanups (as he did in Texas as governor there before becoming president).

Every year millions of cases of cancer, emphysema, neurological disorders, and other conditions caused by corporate pollution—cases like my dad's—are paid for in whole or in part by government-funded programs. From Medicare and Medicaid to government subsidies of hospitals, universities, and research institutions, these programs are funded by tax dollars through the National Institutes of Health (NIH) and the National Institute of Mental Health (NIMH). Most drugs marketed in the United States were first discovered by taxpayer-funded research at universities.

Because it's well understood that corporations use our tax-funded institutions at least as heavily as citizens do, they've traditionally been taxed at similar rates. For example, the top corporate tax rate in the United States was 48 percent during the Carter administration, down from a peak of 53 percent during the Eisenhower and Kennedy years.

Today it stands at 35 percent despite a May 2001 suggestion by Bush administration Treasury secretary Paul O'Neill that there should be no corporate income tax whatsoever. This was the opening salvo in a very real war to have working people bear *all* the costs of the commons and of governance while the wealthy corporate elite derive most of its benefits.

In a feudal state, historian Ernest Bloch reminds us, "The nobles need not pay taxes."

PROFITS BEFORE PEOPLE

This is anti-democratic feudalism in its most raw and naked form, just as the kings and the nobles of old sucked dry the resources of the people they claimed to own. It's the face of wealth and privilege, of what Jefferson called a "pseudo-aristocracy," that works to its own gain and enrichment regardless of the harm done to the nation, the commons, and We the People.

It is, in its most complete form, the face that would "drown government in a bathtub"; that sneers at the First Amendment by putting up "free-speech zones" for protesters against corporate shills in government; that openly and harshly suggests that those who are poor, unemployed, or underemployed are suffering from character defects. The cons say that China and India are taking our jobs because we are lazy, undereducated, can't compete, and don't try hard enough. The cons work hard to protect the corporate interest but are happy to ignore the public interest.

In the early twentieth century, a famous politician defined the kind of society the cons are creating. This politician advocated "a system of government that exercises a dictatorship of the extreme right, typically through the merging of state and business leadership, together with belligerent nationalism." The politician was Benito Mussolini. The word was *fascism*.[9]

Fascism, feudalism, corporatocracy—call it what you will; corporate-embracing cons are not working for what's best for America or for the interests of the middle class who compose the "We the People" in our democracy. The corporate-run state they embrace might appear "free" and even allow elections, but these are only elections among candidates funded and approved by corporate powers, held on voting machines owned by those corporate powers, and marketed in media controlled by those corporate powers.

The war against the middle class is not just a war against an economic class. It is a war against democracy. It is a war against everything for which America stands.

PART II

Democracy Requires a Middle Class

Since the so-called Reagan revolution cut multimillionaires' income taxes by more than half, wealth has concentrated in America in ways not seen since the Robber Baron Era or, before that, pre-revolutionary colonial times. Meanwhile poverty has exploded, and the middle class is under economic siege.

And now come the new feudal lords—the most wealthy and powerful families in America—lobbying Congress that they should retain their stupefying levels of wealth and the power it brings, generation after generation. They say that democracy doesn't require a strong middle class and that Jefferson was wrong when he said that "overgrown wealth" could be "dangerous to the State." They fight against an inheritance tax because, they say, a permanent, hereditary, aristocratically rich ruling class is actually good for the stability of society.

They are wrong.

Of course family farms and businesses should be protected. And of course people who have worked hard and earned a lot of money should be able to ensure that their children and grandchildren and great-grandchildren will live very comfortably. But we must make sure that we don't end up an oligarchy like so many

Latin American countries, where a handful of superrich families rule their nations and democracy is more show than substance.

The Founders of our republic fought a war against an aristocratic, oligarchic nation and were very clear that they didn't want America to ever degenerate into an oligarchy, an aristocracy, or a feudal kingdom. We must adhere to their vision of an egalitarian, democratic republic—and that requires maintaining a viable middle class.

CHAPTER 4

The Myth of the Greedy Founders

At what point does great wealth in the hands of only a few actually harm democracy, threatening to turn a democratic republic into a feudal oligarchy?

It's a debate we haven't had freely and openly in this nation for nearly a century, but it's a question that's vital to the survival of democracy in America.

In a letter to Joseph Milligan on April 6, 1816, Thomas Jefferson explicitly suggested that if individuals became so rich that their wealth could influence or challenge government, their wealth should be decreased upon their death. He wrote, "If the overgrown wealth of an individual be deemed dangerous to the State, the best corrective is the law of equal inheritance to all in equal degree."

In this he was making the same argument that the Framers of Pennsylvania tried to make when writing the Constitution in 1776. As Kevin Phillips notes in his masterpiece *Wealth and Democracy: A Political History of the American Rich,* a Sixteenth Article to the Pennsylvania Bill of Rights (that was only "narrowly defeated") declared: "An enormous proportion of property vested in a few individuals is dangerous to the rights, and destructive of the common happiness of mankind, and, therefore, every free state hath a right by its laws to discourage the possession of such property."[1]

Unfortunately, many Americans believe that our nation was founded exclusively of, by, and for "rich white men" and that the Constitution had, as its primary purpose, the protection of the superrich. They would have us believe that the Constitution's signers didn't really mean all that flowery talk about liberal democracy in a republican form of government.

But the signers didn't send other people's kids to war, as have two generations of the oligarchic Bush family. Many of the Founders themselves gave up everything, even risking (and losing) their lives, their life's savings, or their own homes and families to conceive and birth this nation.

THE FOUNDERS WERE NOT ARISTOCRATS

The theory of the "greedy white Founders" was first widely advanced by Columbia University professor of history and self-described socialist Charles A. Beard, who in 1913 published a book titled *An Economic Interpretation of the Constitution of the United States.*

Numerous historians—on both the right and the left—have since cited his work as evidence that America was founded solely for the purpose of protecting wealthy interests. His myth unfortunately helps conservatives support ending the estate tax, or "death tax," as "the way the Founders would have wanted things" so that the very richest few can rule America.

Every generation sees the past through the lens of its own time. Beard, writing as the great financial robber baron empires of Rockefeller, Gould, Mellon, and Carnegie were being solidified, looked back at the Framers of the Constitution and imagined he was seeing an earlier, albeit smaller, version of his own day's history.

But Beard was wrong.

The majority of the signers of the Constitution were actually acting against their own best economic interests when they put their signatures on that document, just as had the majority of the signers of the Declaration of Independence.

Beard thought he saw his own era's robber barons among the colonial economic elite. And had the American Revolution not happened, he might have been right. But during and after the Revolutionary War, the great fortunes loyal to the Crown fled or were dispersed; and while some of the wealthy British families of 1776 still hold hereditary seats in the British House of Lords, nobody can point to a Rockefeller-dynasty equivalent that survived colonial times in the United States.

While there were some in America among the Founders and the Framers who owned a lot of land, Pulitzer Prize–winning author Bernard Bailyn suggests in his brilliant book *To Begin the World Anew: The Genius and Ambiguities of the American Founders* that they couldn't hold a candle to the true aristocrats of England. With page after page of photographs and old paintings of the homes of the Founders and the Framers, Bailyn shows that none of those who created this nation were rich by European standards.

After an artful and thoughtful comparison of American and British estates, Bailyn concludes bluntly: "There is no possible correspondence, no remote connection, between these provincial dwellings and the magnificent showplaces of the English nobility."[2] After showing and describing to his reader the mansions of the families of power in eighteenth-century Europe, Bailyn writes: "There is nothing in the American World to compare with this."

In *Wealth and Democracy,* Phillips notes that "George Washington, one of the richest Americans, was no more than a wealthy squire in British terms." Phillips says that it wasn't until the 1790s—a generation after the War of Independence—that the first American accumulated a fortune that would be worth 1 million of today's dollars. The Founders and the Framers were, at best, what today would be called the upper-middle-class in terms of lifestyle, assets, and disposable income.

Even Charles and Mary Beard granted that wealth and land ownership were different things. Land, after all, didn't have the scarcity it does today and thus didn't have the same value. Just about any free man could find land to settle, albeit where Native Americans had been decimated by disease or displaced by war.

In fact, with his Louisiana Purchase adding hundreds of millions of acres to America, Jefferson even guaranteed that the value of his own main asset—his land—and that of most of his peers would drop for the next several generations.

When George Washington wrote his will and freed his slaves on his deathbed, he didn't have enough assets to buy the slaves his wife had inherited and free them as well. Like Jefferson, who died in bankruptcy, Washington was "rich" in land but poor in cash.

In 1958 one of America's great professors of history, Forrest McDonald, published an extraordinary book debunking Charles Beard's 1913 hypothesis that the Constitution was created of, by, and for rich white men. McDonald's book, *We the People: The Economic Origins of the Constitution,* bluntly states that Beard's "economic interpretation of the Constitution does not work."[3]

Over the course of more than four hundred meticulously researched pages, McDonald goes back to original historical records and reveals who was promoting and who was opposing the new Constitution and why. He is the first and only historian to do this type of original-source research, and his conclusions are startling.

McDonald notes that a quarter of all the delegates to the Constitutional Convention had voted in their own state legislatures for laws that would have helped debtors and the poor and thus harmed the interests of the rich. "These [bankruptcy/debt relief laws] were the very kinds of laws which, according to Beard's hypothesis, the delegates had convened to prevent," says McDonald. He adds: "Another fourth of the delegates had important economic interests that were adversely affected, directly and immediately, by the Constitution they helped write."

While Beard theorized that the Framers of the Constitution were largely drawn from the class of wealthy bankers and businessmen, McDonald showed that "the most common and by far the most important property holdings of the delegates were not, as Beard has asserted, mercantile, manufacturing, and public security investments, but agricultural property." Most were farmers or plantation owners, and owning a lot of land did not make one rich in those days.

"Finally," McDonald concludes, "it is abundantly evident that the delegates, once inside the convention, behaved as anything but a consolidated economic group."

McDonald then goes into an exhaustive and detailed state-by-state analysis of the state constitutional ratifying conventions that finally brought the U.S. Constitution into law. For example, in Delaware, which voted for ratification,

> almost 77 percent of the delegates were farmers, more than two-thirds of them small farmers with incomes ranging from 75 cents to $5.00 a week. Only slightly more than 23 percent of the delegates were professional men—doctors, judges, and lawyers. None of the delegates was a merchant, manufacturer, banker, or speculator in western lands.

In other states similar numbers showed up. Of the New Jersey delegates supporting ratification, 64.1 percent were small farmers.

In Maryland "the opponents of ratification included from three to six times as large a proportion of merchants, lawyers, and investors in shipping, confiscated estates, and manufacturing as did the delegates who favored ratification."

In South Carolina it was those in economic distress who carried the day: "No fewer than 82 percent of the debtors and borrowers of paper money in the convention voted for ratification." In New Hampshire "of the known farmers in the convention 68.7 percent favored ratification."

But did farmers support the Constitution because they were slave owners or the wealthiest of the landowners, as Beard had guessed back in 1913?

McDonald shows that this certainly was not the case in northern states like New Hampshire and New Jersey, which were not slave states. But what about Virginia and North Carolina, the two largest slaveholding states, asks McDonald rhetorically. Were their plantation owners favoring the Constitution because it protected their economic and slaveholding interests?

"The opposite is true," writes McDonald.

> In both states the wealthy planters—those with personality interests [slaves] as well as those without personality interests—were divided approximately equally on the issue of ratification. In North Carolina small farmers and debtors were likewise equally divided, and in Virginia the great mass of the small farmers and a large majority of the debtors favored ratification.

After dissecting the results of the ratification votes state by state, McDonald sums up: "Beard's thesis . . . is entirely incompatible with the facts."

Voting for Democracy

So what did motivate the Framers of the Constitution?

Along with the answer to this question, we may find the answer to another question historians have asked for two centuries: Why was the Constitutional Convention held in secret, behind locked doors; and why did James Madison not publish his own notes of the convention until 1840, just after the last of the other participants died?

The reason, simply put, was that most of the wealthy men among the delegates were betraying the interests of their own economic class. They were voting for democracy instead of oligarchy. They were voting to create and maintain a middle class instead of creating a nation of, by, and for the rich.

As with any political body, a few of the delegates, "a dozen at the outside," according to McDonald, "clearly acted according to the dictates of their personal economic interests."

But there were larger issues at stake.

The people who hammered out the Constitution had such a strong feeling of history and destiny that it at times overwhelmed them. Their writings show that they truly believed they were doing sacred work—something greater than themselves, their personal interests, and even the narrow interests of their wealthy constituents back in their home states.

Because they traced their ancestry to Europe, the Founders believed they were altering the course of world history. In the entire history of Europe, there had been but one democracy, in Athens, and then only for a few centuries. The Founders believed that if they could marry to European civilization the sort of democracy they had found among the Iroquois, they could truly create a better world.

Thus the secrecy, the locked doors, the intensity of the Constitutional Convention. And thus the willingness to set aside economic interest to produce a document—admittedly imperfect— that would establish an enduring beacon of liberty for the world.

As George Washington, who presided over the Constitutional Convention, wrote to the nation on September 17, 1787, when "transmitting the Constitution" to the people of the new nation: "In all our deliberations on this subject we kept steadily in our view, that which appears to us the greatest interest of every true American, the consolidation of our Union, in which is involved our prosperity, felicity, safety, perhaps our national existence."

SETTING BRUSHFIRES IN THE MINDS OF MEN

The Founders' decision to create a democracy in America was not easy. As John Quincy Adams said, "Posterity—you will never know how much it has cost my generation to preserve your freedom. I hope you will make good use of it."

America was an experiment, and the rest of the "civilized" world assumed it would fail. The Founders not only had to fight for independence from England, they had to convince their peers in Europe that their theory of government could work.

They were a tiny group, and the British Empire was very large. How did they succeed?

Samuel Adams, the tavern owner in Boston who was instrumental in stirring up the Boston Tea Party, said, "It does not take a majority to prevail. But rather an irate, tireless minority, keen on setting brushfires of freedom in the minds of men."

That's who the Founders were and what they did. They were revolutionaries who knew that a vital democracy lay in supporting the middle class and minimizing corporate power. And that's what we must be and what we must do.

CHAPTER 5

Thomas Paine against the Freeloaders

Most Americans these days don't remember why (or when) we instituted a progressive income tax or why taxes even matter in society beyond the obvious issue of paying the cost of government functions like police and fire departments. They don't realize that the Founders of our republic had a visceral and intense concern about multigenerational accumulated wealth and the ability of great wealth to corrupt democracy itself.

Americans today know that none of the supposedly "rich" founders left great fortunes. The foundations that bear the names of people who lived in the late-nineteenth and twentieth centuries are the likes of the Rockefeller Foundation and the Ford Foundation. There is no Jefferson Foundation or Madison Foundation. Americans know this—but they don't know why.

Most Americans also don't realize that a middle class is created and maintained by direct intervention in the marketplace by a democratic government, including laws protecting labor, defining minimum wage, and taxing great wealth.

Without these progressive laws, America would revert to what it looked like during the Robber Baron Era—the average worker earning the equivalent of around $10,000 a year in today's dollars and a wealthy elite so rich and powerful that every branch of government was under its direct or indirect control.

America's first middle class was based on land and the family farm—the agricultural nation that Thomas Jefferson idealized. That began to disintegrate after the Civil War, when the railroads were so omnipresent that they made it possible for large corporations to determine grain prices and drive small farmers out of business.

The Gilded Age that followed produced a progressive backlash, starting with the eruptions of the Grange Movement; it continued with the legislative work of the Progressive Movement of the late nineteenth and early twentieth centuries that brought us direct election of the Senate, the right of women to vote, laws protecting the right to unionize, the estate tax, and a progressive income tax.

These all set the stage for the second American middle class, which finally emerged when Franklin Roosevelt further raised income tax rates on the superrich to 90 percent and created the social safety net we know as Social Security. The middle class also benefited from the anti-poverty programs introduced a generation later by Lyndon Johnson, including Medicare, housing assistance, and food stamps.

A lot of folks believe that these pro–middle class policies were thought up in the twentieth century, but it was actually Thomas Paine who first developed these themes in their modern political context. He did so in his book *The Rights of Man.*

RESCUING PAINE FROM OBSCURITY

Thomas Edison is largely responsible for our knowledge today of Thomas Paine and his writings. In July 1925 Edison rescued Paine from the dustbin of historic obscurity when he wrote a widely read plea to return Paine to the public schools:

> Tom Paine has almost no influence on present-day thinking in the United States because he is unknown to the average citizen. Perhaps I might say right here that this is a national loss and a

deplorable lack of understanding concerning the man who first proposed and first wrote those impressive words, "the United States of America." But it is hardly strange. Paine's teachings have been debarred from schools everywhere and his views of life misrepresented until his memory is hidden in shadows, or he is looked upon as of unsound mind.

We never had a sounder intelligence in this Republic. He was the equal of Washington in making American liberty possible. Where Washington performed Paine devised and wrote. The deeds of one in the Weld were matched by the deeds of the other with his pen.

Washington himself appreciated Paine at his true worth. Franklin knew him for a great patriot and clear thinker. He was a friend and confidant of Jefferson, and the two must often have debated the academic and practical phases of liberty.

I consider Paine our greatest political thinker. As we have not advanced, and perhaps never shall advance, beyond the Declaration and Constitution, so Paine has had no successors who extended his principles. Although the present generation knows little of Paine's writings, and although he has almost no influence upon contemporary thought, Americans of the future will justly appraise his work. I am certain of it.

Thomas Edison was successful in moving the writings of Thomas Paine into the mainstream of American education, influencing a generation that a decade later brought us the many progressive reforms of the 1930s.

An Odd Couple

Thomas Paine wrote *The Rights of Man* as an answer to a debate he was having with Sir Edmund Burke, the famous British nobleman who is revered by modern conservatives (such as Russell Kirk, Barry Goldwater, and William F. Buckley Jr.) as the founder of modern conservative thought. In some ways it's a classic debate between conservative and liberal worldviews, with Paine presenting the liberal side of the equation.

Although modern conservatives like to say that Burke was occasionally progressive in some of his opinions, it was a progressivism that never threatened his lifestyle or that of his wealthy and powerful British peers. He'd come around to supporting American independence, although he was skeptical of our potential for survival without an aristocratic class; he supported the British takeover of India through the East India Company but felt that British rule should be "benevolent" and so prosecuted a man who had "abused" Indian citizens (that trial was similar to the show-trial of Sgt. Charles Grainer for the tortures committed at Abu Ghraib—blame the soldier and not civilian command or national policy); as an Irishman, Burke supported Irish emancipation.

But in his heart and soul, Burke was a staunch supporter of the sort of hierarchical government that Paine rails against in *The Rights of Man.*

Burke and Paine were acquainted. After the Revolutionary War, Paine had returned to England, where he was hailed as the best-selling author of *Common Sense* and *Crisis* ("These are the times that try men's souls") and heralded as one of the true fathers of the American Revolution. (It would not be an exaggeration to say that without Paine there may not have been a Revolution.) Paine had stayed at Burke's home, and the two corresponded.

When the French Revolution broke out, Paine went to France where, despite the fact that he spoke hardly a word of French (he'd dropped out of school at age twelve), he was elected to the National Convention. He was initially fortunate to be in France because during this time *The Rights of Man* was published in England, and the book was considered so radical that Paine was tried and convicted in absentia for seditious libel against the Crown.

But then he publicly crossed swords with Maximilien Robespierre and suggested that King Louis XVI and Marie

Antoinette should be exiled to America. For this he was sentenced to the guillotine and thrown into prison.

It was in prison that Paine wrote his book promoting deism and attacking organized religion, *The Age of Reason*. That book so infuriated churchgoing Americans that when Paine later escaped France and returned to America, he died in obscurity in Greenwich Village, with only six people attending his funeral. As Thomas Edison wrote,

> His Bible was the open face of nature, the broad skies, the green hills. He disbelieved the ancient myths and miracles taught by established creeds. But the attacks on those creeds—or on persons devoted to them—have served to darken his memory, casting a shadow across the closing years of his life. . . . If Paine had ceased his writings with *The Rights of Man* he would have been hailed today as one of the two or three outstanding figures of the Revolution. But *The Age of Reason* cost him glory at the hands of his countrymen—a greater loss to them than to Tom Paine.

BURKE'S WORLDVIEW

Sir Edmund Burke promoted the worldview that animates today's cons: that people are essentially evil and need a strong external controlling force to prevent them from acting out their evil nature; that such a force should most appropriately come from those who have inherited or lawfully obtained wealth, religious power, or political power; and that a permanent large underclass with little power and a permanent small overclass with great power will produce the greatest social good because it will ensure social stability.

In 1790, following up on his conversations with Paine, Burke wrote a letter/pamphlet titled "Reflections on the Revolution in France." In it Burke laid out some of his most important philosophical points, many of which are still quoted by American cons. Burke in particular noted his belief in the danger of true democracy:

> The occupation of an hair-dresser, or of a working tallow-chandler [candle maker], cannot be a matter of honour to any person to say nothing of a number of other more servile employments. Such descriptions of men ought not to suffer oppression from the state; but the state suffers oppression, if such as they, either individually or collectively, are permitted to rule. In this you think you are combating prejudice, but you are at war with nature.

This so incensed Paine that he had to respond, and that response is the book *The Rights of Man.*

PAINE'S DEFENSE OF DEMOCRACY

Paine has such a terrific argument in defense of democracy and self-government that it is worth quoting at length:

> When I contemplate the natural dignity of man, when I feel (for Nature has not been kind enough to me to blunt my feelings) for the honour and happiness of its character, I become irritated at the attempt to govern mankind by force and fraud, as if they were all knaves and fools, and can scarcely avoid disgust at those who are thus imposed upon.

> We have now to review the governments which arise out of society, in contradistinction to those which arose out of superstition and conquest.

> It has been thought a considerable advance towards establishing the principles of Freedom to say that Government is a compact between those who govern and those who are governed; but this cannot be true, because it is putting the effect before the cause; for as man must have existed before governments existed, there necessarily was a time when governments did not exist, and consequently there could originally exist no governors to form such a compact with.

The fact therefore must be that the individuals themselves, each in his own personal and sovereign right, entered into a compact with each other to produce a government: and this is the only mode in which governments have a right to arise, and the only principle on which they have a right to exist.

To possess ourselves of a clear idea of what government is, or ought to be, we must trace it to its origin. In doing this we shall easily discover that governments must have arisen either out of the people or over the people.

Mr. Burke has made no distinction. He investigates nothing to its source, and therefore he confounds everything. . . . As he thus renders it a subject of controversy by throwing the gauntlet, I take him upon his own ground. It is in high challenges that high truths have the right of appearing; and I accept it with the more readiness because it affords me, at the same time, an opportunity of pursuing the subject with respect to governments arising out of society.

Burke strongly defended rule by the rich, enforced by corporate and chartered state power. He wrote:

Let those large proprietors be what they will, and they have their chance of being amongst the best, they are at the very worst, the ballast in the vessel of the commonwealth. For though hereditary wealth, and the rank which goes with it, are too much idolized by creeping sycophants, and the blind abject admirers of power, they are too rashly slighted in shallow speculations of the petulant, assuming, short-sighted coxcombs of philosophy.

Some decent regulated pre-eminence, some preference (not exclusive appropriation) given to birth, is neither unnatural, nor unjust, nor impolitic.

In short, Burke advocated for hereditary wealth and the rights of the aristocracy. Paine, of course, as a small-*d* democrat, was violently against aristocracy. But more than that, Paine saw into the future and realized that the modern aristocracy might in fact be a corporatocracy.

CORPORATE "RIGHTS" ARE A PERVERSION

Paine moved to head off the possibility of an American corporatocracy by insisting that neither government nor corporations
should have rights. Rights, he argued, belong only to the people.
In this regard the last chapter of *The Rights of Man* is perhaps the
most important. Paine wrote:

> I begin with charters and corporations.
>
> It is a perversion of terms to say that a charter gives rights. It
> operates by a contrary effect—that of taking rights away.
>
> Rights are inherently in all the inhabitants; but charters, by an-
> nulling those rights, in the majority, leave the right, by exclusion,
> in the hands of a few. . . . [They] consequently are instruments
> of injustice.
>
> But charters and corporations have a more extensive evil effect
> than what relates merely to elections. They are sources of endless
> contentions in the places where they exist, and they lessen the
> common rights of national society. . . . This species of feudality
> is kept up to aggrandise the corporations at the ruin of towns;
> and the effect is visible.

It is on this most fundamental question, the question of
whether corporations have any role in government, that the difference between us and the cons becomes clear. Thomas Paine,
and all of us who see ourselves in his proud tradition, believe that
government belongs to We the People.

But the cornerstone of the cons' philosophy is the belief that
control of government by a corporate elite and those with inherited wealth will ensure a stable society. It's the core of Reagan's
"greed is good" philosophy that led Republicans in the 1980s to
stop enforcing antitrust laws and to lower taxes on the superrich.
In this Burke was equally consistent:

> The power of perpetuating our property in our families is one
> of the most valuable and interesting circumstances belonging

to it, and that which tends the most to the perpetuation of society itself. It makes our weakness subservient to our virtue; it grafts benevolence even upon avarice. The possessors of family wealth, and of the distinction which attends hereditary possession (as most concerned in it) are the natural securities for this transmission.

In short Burke argued that a stable society depends on inherited wealth. The theory is that because the same rich and powerful people will always control government, laws and customs will hardly ever change. Burke was against change. Because he lived in a monarchy, you can say that Burke himself was not a con but a true conservative—he wanted to "conserve" the aristocratic past of the society in which he lived.

TAX THE RICH, NOT THE POOR

Anyone who calls himself a small-*d* democrat should have a problem with Burke's brand of conservatism. It's a con game to suggest that Americans should want to "conserve" the rule of the rich.

Paine's rebuttal to Burke was to propose what he called "progressive taxation." The last chapter of *The Rights of Man* has several tables, showing specifically how the more wealthy an estate is, the more heavily it should be taxed. Paine pointed out that most of the taxes then paid in England were consumption taxes, such as sales taxes, which fell most heavily on the working class and the poor while the vast land holdings of the wealthy were relatively free of taxes. In essence the wealthy were freeloaders, getting and staying rich off the labor and the taxes of the poor. Paine wrote:

> Before the coming of the Hanoverians, the taxes were divided in nearly equal proportions between the land and articles of consumption, the land bearing rather the largest share: but since that era nearly thirteen millions annually of new taxes have been thrown upon consumption. The consequence of which has been a constant increase in the number and wretchedness of the

poor, and in the amount of the poor-rates. Yet here again the burthen does not fall in equal proportions on the aristocracy with the rest of the community. Their residences, whether in town or country, are not mixed with the habitations of the poor. They live apart from distress, and the expense of relieving it.

Much like today, corporations and the superrich paid relatively little in taxes as a percentage of their assets. Back then most taxes were sales taxes, that is, taxes on consumption; the poor cannot afford sales taxes as well as the rich, so the poor are hurt more by them.

Progressive taxation, Paine said, would cure both the problem of inherited wealth's corrupting government and the continuous drag of taxes on the working class and the poor. He writes that his intended tax would be "lighter" on "small and middling estates . . . It is not till after seven or eight thousand [pounds] a year that it begins to be heavy. The object is not so much the product of the tax as the justice of the measure. The aristocracy has screened itself [from taxes] too much, and this serves to restore a part of the lost equilibrium." That is, the progressive income tax is designed to serve as a way of making sure the aristocrats pay their fair share.

A progressive tax, Paine goes on to argue, would be fairer than sales taxes (which were called "excise laws" or "duties" back then). To demonstrate why sales taxes are unfair, he describes a specific tax that was levied in his time on beer brewed for sale; we have the same sort of tax today, as most states levy a liquor tax. But there was a significant difference between our liquor tax and the beer tax of the eighteenth century. Paine explains:

> The aristocracy do not purchase beer brewed for sale, but brew their own beer free of the duty, and if any commutation at that time were necessary, it ought to have been at the expense of those for whom the exemptions from those services were intended; instead of which, it was thrown on an entirely different class of men.

A landed aristocrat would have had his own winery, his own brewery, his own livestock operation, and so forth. Because the rich could afford to brew their own beer, the beer levy taxed only the poor. The rich were essentially exempt.

One function of the progressive tax is simply to level the playing field, making sure that if the poor are paying more than their fair share through sales tax, at least the rich pay their fair share through income tax. But that's not the main reason for a progressive tax.

THE FIRST ESTATE TAX

"The chief object of this progressive tax (besides the justice of rendering taxes more equal than they are)," Paine wrote, "is, as already stated, to extirpate the overgrown influence arising from the unnatural law of primogeniture [inheritance], and which is one of the principal sources of corruption at elections." Paine knew that if the rich were allowed to pass all their wealth to their heirs, the dynasties that formed would easily take over and corrupt the government.

For that reason Paine argued not just for a progressive tax but for the adoption of an inheritance tax. He pointed out that "hereditary succession is in its nature an absurdity because it is impossible to make wisdom hereditary." He believed that the accumulation of wealth in specific families was anti-democratic. "The earth is an inheritance to all God's children," he wrote.

Burke, of course, saw things differently. He was not fond of the poor. He was a strong believer in the conservative dictum, badly misappropriating and twisting the meaning of Jesus' words, that "The poor you always have with you." How dare the working-class "many" think of taxing the rich "few"? It would threaten Burke's beloved aristocracy and therefore threaten the very core of society. He wrote:

It is said that twenty-four millions ought to prevail over two hundred thousand. True; if the constitution of a kingdom be a problem of arithmetic. This sort of discourse does well enough with the lamp-post for its second: to men who may reason calmly, it is ridiculous. The will of the many, and their interest, must very often differ; and great will be the difference when they make an evil choice.

Today we hear what is essentially a version of that argument. Cons now call the estate tax a "death tax" and claim that it unfairly deprives the wealthy of their property rights.

But we don't have a landed gentry in the United States. There is a certain point—and we approached it in the Gilded Age with the Morgans and the Du Ponts—when family fortunes become so large that they could wield power greater than local government and even the federal government. They became, as Jefferson warned, "a threat to democracy itself." Paine agreed. He believed that it was necessary to limit inherited wealth so as not to create a new feudalism.

CREATING WEALTH FOR ALL

Paine thought that the best way to build a strong democracy was to use his tax on the wealthy to give the poor bootstraps by which they could pull themselves up. He proposed helping out young families with the expense of raising children (a forerunner to our income tax exemptions for dependents), a fund to provide housing and food for the poor (a forerunner to housing vouchers and food stamps), and a reliable and predictable pension for all workers in their old age (a forerunner to Social Security). He also suggested that all nations reduce their armaments by 90 percent to ensure world peace.

Summarizing, Paine noted:

> When it shall be said in any country in the world, my poor are happy; neither ignorance nor distress is to be found among

them; my jails are empty of prisoners, my streets of beggars; the aged are not in want, the taxes are not oppressive; the rational world is my friend, because I am the friend of its happiness: when these things can be said, then may that country boast its constitution and its government.

This, Paine hoped, was the fate of America. And, he believed, when our nation had achieved such an egalitarian and liberal way of life, other nations of the world would naturally emulate us. He predicted that Burke's beloved "benevolent rule by the rich" was doomed to the ash heaps of history.

Unfortunately, that didn't happen. It took America more than 150 years before Franklin Roosevelt—who said he was inspired by Thomas Paine—would implement the majority of Paine's ideas. They worked. The middle class grew. And then the so-called Reagan revolution undid so much of the good that had been done.

The freeloaders are back.

CHAPTER 6

Taxation without Representation

This is not the first time Americans have been screwed.

The American colonists were screwed, too. By the 1700s the colonists living in America should have been well off. Once they had chased away or killed the Native Americans (also screwed), they had plenty of land. Trade was booming. Small businesses were springing up in cities all over the East Coast. A young kid like Benjamin Franklin, coming from modest means, could be apprenticed to a tradesman and hope to easily stay in the middle class.

But by the 1750s, folks realized that something was terribly wrong. The harder they worked, the less money they had. Instead of living in a democracy, they found that their country was run by King George II, and he saw it as a great cash cow—for himself and his wealthy cronies.

King George set the rules of business in America. He levied sales taxes (called "excise laws") on almost every product Americans consumed. To make matters worse, he added import taxes ("duties") on the items Americans brought in from overseas.

The colonists had achieved a middle-class lifestyle, and, as history shows, this will always lead people to try to institute democracy. The colonists pushed for this—at least locally—and tried to reason with King George through their appointed rulers. They tried to democratically elect representatives to talk with the local governors, but King George disbanded their elected assemblies. Instead, in areas where protest was especially strong, the king dispatched spies to haul off protestors without warrant and hold them in jail without trial. In some cases protestors would be taken overseas to King George's own version of Guantánamo.

Kings do that sort of thing.

What really riled the colonists, however, was not just King George's exercise of arbitrary power. It was that he wielded that power to enrich a private corporation—the most anti-democratic of institutions—and one that was actively working against the interests of the emerging American middle class.

The American Revolution began as a revolt against the corporatocracy of the 1700s.

WHEN TEA WAS A MONOPOLY POWER

The American colonialists drank a lot of tea. It was their drug of choice, much as coffee is today. And it was owned by a monopoly.

Conventional wisdom has it that the Tea Act of 1773—a tax law passed in London that led to the Boston Tea Party—was simply an increase in the taxes on tea paid by American colonists. In reality, however, the Tea Act gave what was then the world's largest transnational corporation—the East India Company—full and unlimited access to the American tea trade, and it exempted the company from having to pay taxes to Britain on tea exported to the American colonies. It even gave the company a *tax refund* on millions of pounds of tea it was holding in inventory, unable to sell.

The primary purpose of the Tea Act was to increase the profitability of the East India Company to its stockholders (which included King George III and the wealthy elite that kept him secure in power) and to help the company drive its colonial small-business competitors out of business. Because the company no longer had to pay high taxes to England and held a monopoly on the tea it sold in the American colonies, it was able to lower its prices to undercut those of the local tea importers and the mom-and-pop merchants and tea houses in every town in America.

This infuriated the independence-minded American colonists, who were wholly unappreciative of their colonies' being used as a profit center for the world's largest multinational corporation. They resented that their small businesses still had to pay the higher, pre–Tea Act taxes without having any say or vote in the matter (thus the cry of "No taxation without representation!"). Even in the official British version of the history, the Tea Act of 1773 was a "legislative maneuver by the British ministry of Lord North to make English tea marketable in America" with a goal of helping the financially troubled East India Company quickly "sell 17 million pounds of tea stored in England."[1]

NO TAX CUTS WITHOUT REPRESENTATION

The battle between the small businessmen of America and the huge multinational East India Company actually began in Pennsylvania, according to one observer. "At Philadelphia," he writes, "those to whom the teas of the [East India] Company were intended to be consigned, were induced by persuasion, or constrained by menaces, to promise, on no terms, to accept the proffered consignment."

Resistance was organizing and growing, and the Tea Act marked the boiling point. The colonists were preparing to throw off a corporation that for almost two hundred years had determined nearly every aspect of their lives through its economic and political power. They were planning to destroy its goods, intimidate its employees, and face down the guns of the government that supported it.

A pamphlet called *The Alarm*, signed by an enigmatic "Rusticus," circulated through the colonies. One issue made clear the feelings of colonial Americans about England's largest transnational corporation and its behavior around the world:

> Are we in like Manner to be given up to the Disposal of the East India Company, who have now the Assurance, to step forth in Aid of the Minister, to execute his Plan, of enslaving America? Their Conduct in Asia, for some Years past, has given simple Proof, how little they regard the Laws of Nations, the Rights, Liberties, or Lives of Men. . . . Fifteen hundred Thousands, it is said, perished by Famine in one Year, not because the Earth denied its Fruits; but [because] this Company and their Servants engulfed all the Necessaries of Life, and set them at so high a Rate that the poor could not purchase them.

The pamphleteering worked. The tea ships were turned back at harbors in Pennsylvania and New York. Then, on a cold November evening, they arrived in Boston. The next morning the following notice was widely circulated:

> Friends, Brethren, Countrymen! That worst of plagues, the detested TEA, has arrived in this harbour. The hour of destruction, a manly opposition to the machinations of tyranny, stares you in the face. Every friend to his country, to himself, and to posterity, is now called upon to meet in Faneuil Hall, at nine o'clock, this day, at which time the bells will ring, to make a united and successful resistance to this last, worst, and most destructive measure of administration.

The reaction to the pamphlet—an example of what was truly a "free press" in America—was emphatic. People came to the meeting place from within the city and from neighboring towns. Those who assembled in Boston faced the same issue that citizens who oppose combined corporate and co-opted government power all over the world confront today: Should they take on a well-financed and heavily armed opponent when such resistance could lead to their own imprisonment or death? Even worse, what if they lost the struggle, leading to the imposition on them and their children of an even more repressive regime to support the profits of the corporation?

The citizens chose to act. They threw 342 chests of tea—valued at 9,659 pounds sterling or, in today's currency, just over a million U.S. dollars—overboard in an act of protest they called the Boston Tea Party.

In response, the British Parliament passed the Boston Port Act, which stated that Boston's port would be closed until its citizens reimbursed the East India Company for the tea they'd destroyed. The colonists refused.

A year and a half later, the colonists again openly stated their defiance of the East India Company and Great Britain by taking on British troops in an armed conflict at Lexington and Concord ("the shot heard 'round the world") on April 19, 1775.

They explained their action in 1776 in the document they titled the Declaration of Independence. Among their reasons for separating America from Britain: "For cutting off our Trade with all parts of the world: For imposing Taxes on us without our Consent." The British had used tax and anti-smuggling laws to make it nearly impossible for American small businesses to compete against the huge East India Company, and the Tea Act of 1773 was the last straw.

LIMITING CORPORATE POWER

Once the Revolutionary War was over and the Constitution had been worked out and presented to the states for ratification, Thomas Jefferson turned his attention to what he and James Madison felt was a terrible inadequacy in the new Constitution: it didn't explicitly stipulate the "natural rights" of the new nation's citizens, and it didn't protect against the rise of new commercial monopolies like the East India Company.

On December 20, 1787, Jefferson wrote to Madison about these concerns. He said, bluntly, that the Constitution was deficient in several areas, including "restriction of monopolies." Madison agreed and joined Jefferson in pushing for a law, which, as they wrote it, would "ban monopolies in commerce."

Although Jefferson was specifically talking about corporations using copyright laws to monopolize marketplaces for intellectual properties, it was part of a broader effort by many of the Founders to prevent anything like an East India Company from ever arising in America again. As part of that effort, the states passed hundreds of laws restricting and restraining corporations.

Wisconsin, for example, passed a law that stated:

> No corporation doing business in this state shall pay or contribute, or offer consent or agree to pay or contribute, directly or indirectly, any money, property, free service of its officers or employees or thing of value to any political party, organization, committee or individual for any political purpose whatsoever, or for the purpose of influencing legislation of any kind, or to promote or defeat the candidacy of any person for nomination, appointment or election to any political office.

The penalty for any corporate official's violating that law and getting cozy with politicians on behalf of a corporation was five years in prison and a substantial fine.

These laws prevented corporations from harming humans while still allowing people to create their corporations and use them to make money. Everybody won.

THE CORPORATOCRACY STRIKES BACK

In the 1886 *Santa Clara County v. Southern Pacific Railroad* case, the U.S. Supreme Court ruled that the state tax assessor, not the county assessor, had the right to determine the taxable value of fence posts along the railroad's right of way.

In writing up the case's headnote, however—a commentary that has no legal status—the court reporter, a former railroad president named J. C. Bancroft Davis, opened the headnote with the sentence: "The defendant Corporations are persons within the intent of the clause in section 1 of the Fourteen Amendment to the Constitution of the United States, which forbids a State to deny to any person within its jurisdiction the equal protection of the laws." Oddly, the court had ruled no such thing. A handwritten note from Chief Justice Morrison Remick Waite to reporter Davis that we found in the National Archives said: "We avoided meeting the Constitutional question in the decision." And nowhere in the decision itself does the Court say corporations are persons.

Nonetheless, corporate attorneys picked up the language of Davis's headnote and began to quote it like a mantra. Soon the Supreme Court itself, in a stunning display of either laziness (not reading the actual case) or deception (rewriting the Constitution without issuing an opinion or having open debate on the issue), was quoting Davis's headnote in subsequent cases. Although Davis's *Santa Clara* headnote didn't have the force of law, once the Court quoted it as the basis for later decisions its new doctrine of corporate personhood became law.

Prior to 1886 the Bill of Rights and the Fourteenth Amendment defined human rights, and individuals—representing themselves and their own opinions—were free to say and do what they wanted. Corporations, being artificial creations of the states, didn't have rights but instead had privileges. The state in which a corporation was incorporated determined those privileges and how they could be used. And the same, of course, was true for other forms of "legally enacted game playing" such as unions, churches, unincorporated businesses, partnerships, and even governments—all of which have only privileges, not rights.

But with the stroke of his pen, the court reporter moved corporations out of that "privileges" category—leaving behind all the others (unions, governments, and small unincorporated businesses still don't have "rights")—and moved them into the "rights" category with humans, citing the Fourteenth Amendment, which was passed at the end of the Civil War to grant the human right of equal protection under the law to newly freed slaves.

On December 3, 1888, President Grover Cleveland delivered his annual address to Congress. Apparently, the president had taken notice of the *Santa Clara* Supreme Court headnote, its politics, and its consequences, for he said in his speech to the nation, delivered before a joint session of Congress:

> As we view the achievements of aggregated capital, we discover the existence of trusts, combinations, and monopolies, while the citizen is struggling far in the rear or is trampled to death beneath an iron heel. Corporations, which should be the carefully restrained creatures of the law and the servants of the people, are fast becoming the people's masters.

Which brings us to the present.

THE CASE OF *NIKE V. KASKY*

After almost thirty years of conservative economics, America is once again faced with a collection of trusts, combinations, and monopolies that are leaving citizens struggling "far in the rear." This time the corporate conglomerates—big-box retailers, monolithic media, big pharma, and big oil—are making a comeback after having been tamed during the middle of this century.

Call it the Wal-Martization of America—or the death of the American middle class—and with it comes very real danger to the future of democracy.

Corporate monoliths are taking over local politics, reshaping communities, and displacing citizen power with corporate power. An Iowa study showed that small towns lose up to 40 percent of their retail trade after a Wal-Mart moves in. Wal-Mart pays an average of $9.70 per hour, when the U.S. average is $10.25 per hour. Wal-Mart is driving down wages, killing local businesses, and undermining the middle class in America. And Wal-Mart is only the most public of the mega-corporations that are using their monopoly power to change American society.

But what is truly frightening is that the corporatocracy that is taking over the levers of power in our government is lobbying for political rights for the corporate entity itself. Corporations are claiming all the rights of persons, creating another front in the undeclared war on the middle class.

The case of *Nike v. Kasky* tells the whole story. In 2002, while Nike was conducting a huge and expensive PR blitz to tell people that it had cleaned up its subcontractors' sweatshop labor practices, an alert consumer advocate and activist in California named Marc Kasky caught Nike in what he alleges are a number of specific deceptions. Citing a California law that forbids corporations from intentionally deceiving people in their commercial statements, Kasky sued the multibillion-dollar corporation.

Instead of refuting Kasky's charge by proving in court that it didn't lie, however, Nike instead chose to argue that corporations should enjoy the same "free speech" right to deceive that individual human citizens have in their personal lives. If people have the constitutionally protected right to say, "The check is in the mail" or "That looks great on you," Nike's reasoning went, a corporation should have the same right to say whatever it wants in its corporate PR campaigns.

In a *New York Times* column supporting Nike's position, Bob Herbert wrote, "In a real democracy, even the people you disagree with get to have their say."[2]

True enough.

But Nike isn't a person—it's a corporation. Corporations are nonliving, nonbreathing, legal fictions. They feel no pain. They don't need clean water to drink, fresh air to breathe, or healthy food to consume. They can't be put in prison. They can change their identity or appearance in a day, change their citizenship in

an hour, and sever parts of themselves to create entirely new entities. They can live forever. Some have compared corporations to
robots in that they are human creations that can outlive individual
humans, performing their assigned tasks forever.

Nike was asking the courts to declare that this artificial con-
struct—the corporation—had all the rights of a person like you
or me. Why would it want such rights? Not to be a better citizen
of the USA! What it was really asking for—what it stated in plain
language in its brief—was the right to deceive people.

Nike took this argument all the way to the California Supreme
Court, where, in a 2003 decision heard 'round the corporate world,
it lost. Nike then appealed to the U.S. Supreme Court, which
refused to hear the case on the grounds that it hadn't properly
wended its way through the court system. Before going to trial,
however, Nike settled.

It could have tried the case, and, if it lost, gone back to the U.S.
Supreme Court, but most legal analysts agree that Nike thought
it might lose the case and didn't want to test its argument again.
Perhaps the company didn't like the negative press it was getting
in the papers. Perhaps it realized that you can't tell the American
people you intend to deceive them and expect to get away with it.

Corporations R Us

Just because corporate America lost that battle, however, doesn't
mean it lost the war. Corporate America is rising up, and, unlike
you and me, when large corporations speak they can use a billion-
dollar bullhorn.

Of the many pernicious features of the Nike case, perhaps the
most insidious was the support Nike received from the U.S. government. The U.S. solicitor general—the lawyer who is supposed
to represent We the People—joined the case, arguing for Nike. The
U.S. Chamber of Commerce filed a brief on Nike's behalf, arguing

that the effect of the California Supreme Court ruling would be to "suppress corporations' speech" and discriminate against them by holding that speech by corporations on important public policy matters is subject to the reduced protection accorded "commercial speech."

Historically in the United States, we have had a clear line of separation between government and corporate interests. For two hundred years, if corporations gave money to government, that was called bribery. In fact, in 1907 Teddy Roosevelt passed a law saying it's a crime for a corporation to give money to a politician. And that law is still on the books.

When a private interest takes over our government, we have a serious problem: it means the loss of democracy and inevitably leads to a war on the middle class. That's what is happening today.

In 2005 George W. Bush, using your and my tax dollars, sent out official invitations, asking people to attend events in support of the Central American Free Trade Agreement. The president has every right, as a free citizen in a democracy, to say whatever he wants, including saying that corporations should run America. He'd be wrong, but he can say it.

But the event in question was sponsored wholly by private corporations. And the invitation from the White House—paid for with your money—came complete with corporate logos. The White House was using your tax dollars to advertise some of the world's largest multinational corporations.

Have we lost all distinction between government power and corporate power?

Perhaps it's time for another tea party.

CHAPTER 7

James Madison versus the Business of War

On a 2002 visit to Argentina, I found myself in a pleasant, middle-class home, sitting across the table from a woman who had been tortured and electro-shocked by the police for protesting, exactly twenty years earlier, the war between Great Britain and Argentina over the Falkland Islands. I never would have guessed. She was soft-spoken, middle-aged, middle-class, and fashionably dressed. But she was one of "the disappeared"—and among the lucky ones who were released.

"The war covered up the dark side of the government and the corruption of the politicians of the time," another woman in a Buenos Aires restaurant told me. "It was a good way of putting the attention of the people somewhere else, like when you're with a little child, and you want to distract him, and you say, 'Come here and have some sweets.' And we bought that immediately. There was dancing in the streets. 'We're going to win a war—oh boy, oh boy!' We went with flags to the streets, singing the national songs to celebrate the possibility of winning this war."

The Falklands war was over quickly, in part because each side had an enemy: a nation. Terrorism, on the other hand, is not an enemy: it's a tactic. Unless you want to have a perpetual war, you must declare war against an enemy, not a behavior.

But what if a perpetual war is just what the cons want, as another man in a restaurant in Buenos Aires suggested? What if war provides the corporatocracy the best possible means of hiding behind the flag?

HIDING BEHIND THE FLAG

In the novel *1984* by George Orwell, the way a seemingly democratic president kept his nation in a continual state of repression was by having a continuous war. Cynics suggest that the lesson wasn't lost on Lyndon Johnson or Richard Nixon, both of whom, they say, extended the Vietnam War so that it coincidentally ran over election cycles, knowing that a wartime president's party is more likely to be reelected and has more power than a president in peacetime.

Similarly, Hitler used the 1933 burning of the Reichstag (Parliament) building by a deranged Dutchman to declare a "war on terrorism" and establish his legitimacy as a leader (even though he hadn't won a majority in the previous election).

"You are now witnessing the beginning of a great epoch in history," he proclaimed, standing in front of the burned-out building, surrounded by national media. "This fire," he said, his voice trembling with emotion, "is the beginning." He used the occasion—"a sign from God," he called it—to declare an all-out war on terrorism and its ideological sponsors, a people, he said, who traced their origins to the Middle East and found motivation for their "evil" deeds in their religion.

Two weeks later the first prison for terrorists was built in Oranianberg, holding the first suspected allies of the infamous terrorist. In a national outburst of patriotism, the nation's flag was everywhere, even printed in newspapers suitable for display.

Within four weeks of the terrorist attack, in the name of combating terrorism and fighting the philosophy he said spawned it, the nation's now-popular leader had pushed through legislation that suspended constitutional guarantees of free speech, privacy, and habeas corpus. Police could now intercept mail and wiretap phones; suspected terrorists could be imprisoned without specific charges and without access to their lawyers; and police could sneak into people's homes without warrants if the cases involved terrorism.

To get his patriotic "Decree on the Protection of People and State" passed, over the objections of concerned legislators and civil libertarians, Hitler agreed to put a four-year sunset provision on it: if the national emergency provoked by the terrorist attack was over by then, the people's freedoms and rights would be restored and the police agencies would be rerestrained.

Within the first months after that terrorist attack, at the suggestion of a political adviser, Hitler brought a formerly obscure word into common usage. Instead of referring to the nation by its name, he began to refer to it as "the Homeland." As hoped, people's hearts swelled with pride, and the seeds of an us-versus-them mentality were sown. Our land was "the" homeland, citizens thought: all others were simply foreign lands.

Within a year of the terrorist attack, Hitler's advisers determined that the nation's local police and federal agencies lacked the clear communication and overall coordinated administration necessary to deal with the terrorist threat facing the nation, including those citizens who were of Middle Eastern ancestry and thus probably terrorist sympathizers. He proposed a single new national agency to protect the security of the Homeland, consolidating the actions of dozens of previously independent police, border, and investigative agencies under a single powerful leader.

Most Americans remember his Office of Homeland Security (known as the Reichssicherheitshauptamt and Schutzstaffel) simply by its most famous agency's initials: the SS.

Perhaps most important, Hitler invited his supporters in industry into the halls of government to help build his new detention camps, his new military, and his new empire, which was to herald a thousand years of peace. Industry and government worked hand-in-glove in a new type of pseudo-democracy first proposed by Mussolini and sustained by war.

This wasn't a new lesson, however, and neither Orwell nor Hitler was the first to note that a democracy at war was weakened and at risk.

Perpetual War

On April 20, 1795, James Madison, who had just helped shepherd through the Constitution and the Bill of Rights and would become president of the United States in the following decade, wrote, "Of all the enemies to public liberty war is, perhaps, the most to be dreaded because it comprises and develops the germ of every other. War is the parent of armies; from these proceed debts and taxes. And armies, and debts, and taxes are the known instruments for bringing the many under the domination of the few."

Reflecting on war's impact on the executive branch of government, Madison continued his letter about the dangerous and intoxicating power of war for a president:

> In war, too, the discretionary power of the Executive is extended. Its influence in dealing out offices, honors, and emoluments is multiplied; and all the means of seducing the minds, are added to those of subduing the force of the people. The same malignant aspect in republicanism may be traced in the inequality of fortunes, and the opportunities of fraud, growing out of a state of war . . . and in the degeneracy of manners and morals, engendered by both.

"No nation," he concluded, "could preserve its freedom in the midst of continual warfare."

But it's not just Madison's ghost warning us. More-recent presidents have also noted the danger of a corporate usurpation of democracy, particularly when fed by the bloody meat of war.

As he was leaving office, the old warrior President Dwight D. Eisenhower had looked back over his years as president and as a general and supreme commander of the Allied Forces in France during World War II and noted that the Cold War had brought a new, Orwellian type of war to the American landscape—a perpetual war supported by a perpetual war industry. It was the confluence of the two things Jefferson had warned against—and had tried to ban in his first proposed version of the Bill of Rights.

"Our military organization today bears little relation to that known by any of my predecessors in peacetime, or indeed by the fighting men of World War II or Korea," Eisenhower said in sobering tones in a nationally televised speech.

> Until the latest of our world conflicts, the United States had no armaments industry. American makers of plowshares could, with time and as required, make swords as well. But now we can no longer risk emergency improvisation of national defense; we have been compelled to create a permanent armaments industry of vast proportions. Added to this, three and a half million men and women are directly engaged in the defense establishment. We annually spend on military security more than the net income of all United States corporations.

Nonetheless, Eisenhower added,

> This conjunction of an immense military establishment and a large arms industry is new in the American experience. The total influence, economic, political, even spiritual, is felt in every city, every State house, every office of the Federal government. We recognize the imperative need for this development. Yet we must not fail to comprehend its grave implications. Our toil, resources and livelihood are all involved; so is the very structure of our society.

> In the councils of government, we must guard against the acquisition of unwarranted influence, whether sought or unsought, by the military-industrial complex. The potential for the disastrous rise of misplaced power exists and will persist.

Eisenhower concluded with a very specific warning to us, the generation that would follow:

> We must never let the weight of this combination endanger our liberties or democratic processes. We should take nothing for granted. Only an alert and knowledgeable citizenry can compel the proper meshing of the huge industrial and military machinery of defense with our peaceful methods and goals, so that security and liberty may prosper together.

The Business of War

War had become big business in America. Now we not only consume a vast amount of military equipment but we sell it to the world: we're the world's largest exporter of weapons of virtually all sizes and types.

Ever since corporations stole human rights in the *Santa Clara* coup of 1886 and began to first fully exercise them during the Reagan era (and continue today with increasing belligerence), Madison's and Eisenhower's warnings have become more of a concern.

Military spending is the least effective way to help, stimulate, or sustain an economy for a very simple reason: military products are used once and destroyed.

When a government uses taxpayer money to build a bridge or highway or hospital, that investment will be used for decades, perhaps centuries, and will continue to fuel economic activity throughout its lifetime. But when taxpayer dollars are used to build a bomb or a bullet, that military hardware will be used once and then vanish. As it vanishes, so does the wealth it represented, never to be recovered.

As Eisenhower said in an April 1953 speech:

> Every gun that is made, every warship launched, every rocket fired, signifies, in the final sense, a theft from those who hunger and are not fed, those who are cold and are not clothed. The

world in arms is not spending money alone. It is spending the sweat of its laborers, the genius of its scientists, the hopes of its children.

It was a brilliant articulation of human needs in a world increasingly dominated by the nonbreathing entities called corporations whose values are profit and growth—not the human values of fresh air, clean water, pure food, freedom, and happiness. But it was a call unheeded and, today, it is nearly totally forgotten.

ONE WAR, TWO PATHS

Franklin Roosevelt once said, "There is a mysterious cycle in human events. To some generations much is given. Of other generations much is expected. This generation of Americans has a rendezvous with destiny."

Perhaps, as he suggested, history does, indeed, repeat itself.

Today, as we face international financial and domestic political crises, it's useful to remember that the ravages of the Great Depression hit Germany and the United States alike. Through the 1930s, however, Hitler and Roosevelt chose very different courses to bring their nations back to power and prosperity.

Germany's response was to merge corporations into government, creating unequal protection for working citizens, privatizing much of the commons, and creating an illusion of prosperity through continuous and ever-expanding war. America's response was to pass minimum-wage laws, increase taxes on corporations and the wealthiest individuals, establish Social Security, and become the employer of last resort through programs like the WPA to create a vibrant middle class and real prosperity.

One country chose corporatocracy; the other chose democracy and the rule of We the People.

Today James Madison's warning about an executive branch beholden to "commercial monopolies" and intoxicated by war takes on a new and chilling meaning. And to the extent that our Constitution is still intact, the choice is again ours as to which path we'll pursue.

CHAPTER 8

FDR and the Economic Royalists

We have a name for government of, by, and for corporations. It's called *fascism.*

Benito Mussolini, one of the best-known fascists of the twentieth century, claimed to have invented the word. It was actually Italian philosopher Giovanni Gentile who wrote the entry in the *Encyclopedia Italiana* that said: "Fascism should more appropriately be called corporatism because it is a merger of state and corporate power." Mussolini, however, affixed his name to the entry and claimed credit for it.

In 1938 Mussolini realized his vision of fascism when he dissolved Parliament and replaced it with the Camera dei Fasci e delle Corporazioni—the Chamber of the Fascist Corporations. Corporations were still privately owned, but now instead of having to sneak their money to folks like Tom DeLay and covertly write legislation, they were openly in charge of the government.

Franklin Roosevelt's administration was quite aware of the nature of the fascist government. In early 1944 the *New York Times* asked Vice President Henry Wallace (in Wallace's words) "to write a piece answering the following questions: What is a fascist? How many fascists have we? How dangerous are they?"

In April 1944, when Vice President Wallace published his answer in the *Times,* he certainly could point to examples of

Americans who had aligned themselves with Mussolini and Hitler. Wallace notes that "American fascists were clandestinely aligned with their German counterparts before the war, and are even now preparing to resume where they left off, after 'the present unpleasantness' ceases." Indeed, several well-known and powerful Americans—including Prescott Bush, George W.'s granddaddy—lost businesses in the 1940s because of charges by Roosevelt that they were doing business with Hitler.

What concerned Henry Wallace most, however, was not political treason but the possibility that a distinctly American style of fascism could emerge. He wrote:

> The really dangerous American fascists are not those who are hooked up directly or indirectly with the Axis. The FBI has its fingers on those. The dangerous American fascist is the man who wants to do in the United States in an American way what Hitler did in Germany in a Prussian way.

Roosevelt's government came to power in the 1930s in the wake of the Great Depression. He didn't know he was going to fight a war in Europe, but he did plan to fight a war in America—a war on what he called the "economic royalists."

When Roosevelt accepted his party's renomination in 1936 in Philadelphia, he gave a history lesson we could use today (see the transcript on pages 122–128). The American revolutionaries, FDR explained, fought for freedom against political royalty. We won and political royalty lost. The dawning of the modern industrial world of mass production and distribution, however, "combined to bring forward a new civilization and with it, a problem for those who sought to remain free. For out of this modern civilization, economic royalists carved a new dynasty. New kingdoms were built on concentration of control over material things."

The new kings of FDR's day were corporate monopolists: Carnegie, Mellon, Rockefeller, and Du Pont. "These new royals," he continued, "granted that the government could protect the citizen in his right to vote, but they denied that the government could do anything to protect the citizen in his right to work and his right to live."

This is the debate we are returning to in our time. Do we have a right to work, or is it a privilege? Is society organized to encourage business because business will work in a way that will benefit society, or does business operate independent of society?

Roosevelt knew too well that absolute power corrupts absolutely. If the new economic royalty were granted the sway over the economy that they desired, what would prevent them from stopping at economic control? Why not do what the fascists were doing in Mussolini's Italy and try to have it all?

Roosevelt said: "It was natural and perhaps human that the privileged princes of these new economic dynasties, thirsting for power, reached out for control over government itself. They created a new despotism and wrapped it in the robes of legal sanction. . . . And as a result the average man once more confronts the problem that faced the Minute Man."

Ceding economic control to the new economic royalty does not create a "free" market. It creates fascism: the replacement of a democracy of We the People with an economic and political system controlled by the new feudal lords.

IT CAN HAPPEN HERE

In his article for the *New York Times,* Vice President Wallace outlined the Roosevelt administration's concern about the possibility of a particularly American fascism:

> If we define an American fascist as one who in case of conflict puts money and power ahead of human beings, then there are undoubtedly several million fascists in the United States. There are probably several hundred thousand if we narrow the definition to include only those who in their search for money and power are ruthless and deceitful. . . . They are patriotic in time

of war because it is to their interest to be so, but in time of peace they follow power and the dollar wherever they may lead.

Sinclair Lewis imagined just such a corporate takeover of America in his 1935 novel, *It Can't Happen Here.* In Lewis's novel a conservative southern politician is helped to the presidency by a nationally syndicated radio talk-show host. The politician— Berzelius "Buzz" Windrip—runs his campaign on family values, the flag, and patriotism. Windrip and the talk-show host portray advocates of traditional American democracy as anti-American. When Windrip becomes president, he opens a Guantánamo-style detention center; and the viewpoint character of the book, Vermont newspaper editor Doremus Jessup, flees to Canada to avoid prosecution under new "patriotic" laws that make it illegal to criticize the president.

As Lewis noted in his novel,

> the President, with something of his former good-humor [said]: "There are two [political] parties, the Corporate and those who don't belong to any party at all, and so, to use a common phrase, are just out of luck!" The idea of the Corporate or Corporative State, Secretary [of State] Sarason had more or less taken from Italy.

And President "Windrip's partisans called themselves the Corporatists, or, familiarly, the 'Corpos,' which nickname was generally used."

Vice President Wallace may have had Lewis's story in mind when he wrote that the fascists are particularly dangerous because, while "paying lip service to democracy and the common welfare, in their insatiable greed for money and the power which money gives, [they] do not hesitate surreptitiously to evade the laws designed to safeguard the public from monopolistic extortion."

Fascists have an agenda that is primarily economic, creating a modern version of feudalism by merging corporate interests with those of the state.

Fascists get richer (and more powerful) on the backs of the middle class. In fascist administrations the locally owned small and medium-sized businesses are replaced by fascist-owned corporations. As Wallace wrote, "Monopolists who fear competition and who distrust democracy because it stands for equal opportunity would like to secure their position against small and energetic enterprise. In an effort to eliminate the possibility of any rival growing up, some monopolists would sacrifice democracy itself."

That's what we are seeing in the United States today. Instead of dissolving the House of Representatives like Mussolini did and replacing them with representatives of major corporations, however, we have people who are elected only because they can buy enough television advertising to get elected, and the only place they can get that kind of money is from the corporations.

LYING TO THE PEOPLE

American fascists—those who would want former CEOs as president, vice president, House majority whip, and Senate majority leader and who would write legislation with corporate interests in mind—don't generally talk to We the People about their real agenda or the harm it does to small businesses and working people. Instead, as Hitler did with the trade union leaders and the Jews, they point to a "them" to pin with blame and distract people from the harms of their economic policies.

In a comment prescient of George W. Bush's suggestion that civilization itself is at risk because of gays, Wallace continued:

> The symptoms of fascist thinking are colored by environment and adapted to immediate circumstances. But always and everywhere they can be identified by their appeal to prejudice and by the desire to play upon the fears and vanities of different groups in order to gain power. It is no coincidence that the growth of modern tyrants has in every case been heralded by the growth of prejudice. It may be shocking to some people in this country

to realize that, without meaning to do so, they hold views in common with Hitler when they preach discrimination.

But Wallace believed that even the techniques of distraction and discrimination would not be enough to convince the people to turn their government over to the corporatocracy. Fascists could gain real power only by lying to the people. Unfortunately, Wallace believed it would be easy for fascists to lie because they controlled the media:

> The American fascists are most easily recognized by their deliberate perversion of truth and fact. Their newspapers and propaganda carefully cultivate every fissure of disunity, every crack in the common front against fascism. They use every opportunity to impugn democracy. . . .
>
> The American fascist would prefer not to use violence. His method is to poison the channels of public information. With a fascist the problem is never how best to present the truth to the public but how best to use the news to deceive the public into giving the fascist and his group more money or more power.

In his strongest indictment of the tide of fascism he saw rising in America, Vice President Wallace added,

> They claim to be super-patriots, but they would destroy every liberty guaranteed by the Constitution. They demand free enterprise, but are the spokesmen for monopoly and vested interest. Their final objective toward which all their deceit is directed is to capture political power so that, using the power of the state and the power of the market simultaneously, they may keep the common man in eternal subjection.

Finally, Wallace said,

> The myth of fascist efficiency has deluded many people. . . . Democracy, to crush fascism internally, must . . . develop the ability to keep people fully employed and at the same time balance the budget. It must put human beings first and dollars second. It must appeal to reason and decency and not to violence

and deceit. We must not tolerate oppressive government or industrial oligarchy in the form of monopolies and cartels.

HIDING BEHIND THE FLAG

Today we again stand at the same crossroad Roosevelt and Wallace confronted during the Great Depression and World War II. Fascism is again rising in America, this time calling itself "compassionate conservatism."

The cons' behavior today eerily parallels the day in 1936 when Roosevelt said, "In vain they seek to hide behind the flag and the Constitution. In their blindness they forget what the flag and the Constitution stand for."

The cons are passing budgets that give billions to private companies to conduct an illegal war on our behalf while cutting money for food for low-income families. They tell us it is unpatriotic to criticize the government, then want to give corporations free-speech rights to lie about their products to the American people. They defend the president for eavesdropping on Americans without a warrant[1] in violation of half the Bill of Rights, but they don't want Americans to know which lobbyists have influenced their votes.

We can't sit on our hands and hope someone else will do something. If our elected representatives don't wake up and reverse course, we will soon no longer recognize the country our Founders created. It's up to us—to We the People—to sound the alarm.

Speech given by Franklin D. Roosevelt upon accepting his party's nomination for a second term at the Democratic National Convention, Philadelphia, Pennsylvania, June 27, 1936.

HERE, and in every community throughout the land, we are met at a time of great moment to the future of the Nation. It is an occasion to be dedicated to the simple and sincere expression of an attitude toward problems, the determination of which will profoundly affect America.

I come not only as a leader of a party, not only as a candidate for high office, but as one upon whom many critical hours have imposed and still impose a grave responsibility.

For the sympathy, help and confidence with which Americans have sustained me in my task I am grateful. For their loyalty I salute the members of our great party, in and out of political life in every part of the Union. I salute those of other parties, especially those in the Congress of the United States who on so many occasions have put partisanship aside. I thank the Governors of the several States, their Legislatures, their State and local officials who participated unselfishly and regardless of party in our efforts to achieve recovery and destroy abuses. Above all I thank the millions of Americans who have borne disaster bravely and have dared to smile through the storm.

America will not forget these recent years, will not forget that the rescue was not a mere party task. It was the concern of all of us. In our strength we rose together, rallied our energies together, applied the old rules of common sense, and together survived.

In those days we feared fear. That was why we fought fear. And today, my friends, we have won against the most dangerous of our foes. We have conquered fear.

Speech given by Franklin D. Roosevelt in 1936 *(continued)*

But I cannot, with candor, tell you that all is well with the world. Clouds of suspicion, tides of ill-will and intolerance gather darkly in many places. In our own land we enjoy indeed a fullness of life greater than that of most Nations. But the rush of modern civilization itself has raised for us new difficulties, new problems which must be solved if we are to preserve to the United States the political and economic freedom for which Washington and Jefferson planned and fought.

Philadelphia is a good city in which to write American history. This is fitting ground on which to reaffirm the faith of our fathers; to pledge ourselves to restore to the people a wider freedom; to give to 1936 as the founders gave to 1776—an American way of life.

That very word freedom, in itself and of necessity, suggests freedom from some restraining power. In 1776 we sought freedom from the tyranny of a political autocracy—from the eighteenth century royalists who held special privileges from the crown. It was to perpetuate their privilege that they governed without the consent of the governed; that they denied the right of free assembly and free speech; that they restricted the worship of God; that they put the average man's property and the average man's life in pawn to the mercenaries of dynastic power; that they regimented the people.

And so it was to win freedom from the tyranny of political autocracy that the American Revolution was fought. That victory gave the business of governing into the hands of the average man, who won the right with his neighbors to make and order his own destiny through his own Government. Political tyranny was wiped out at Philadelphia on July 4, 1776.

Since that struggle, however, man's inventive genius released new forces in our land which reordered the lives of our

Speech given by Franklin D. Roosevelt in 1936 *(continued)*

people. The age of machinery, of railroads; of steam and electricity; the telegraph and the radio; mass production, mass distribution—all of these combined to bring forward a new civilization and with it a new problem for those who sought to remain free.

For out of this modern civilization economic royalists carved new dynasties. New kingdoms were built upon concentration of control over material things. Through new uses of corporations, banks and securities, new machinery of industry and agriculture, of labor and capital—all undreamed of by the fathers—the whole structure of modern life was impressed into this royal service.

There was no place among this royalty for our many thousands of small business men and merchants who sought to make a worthy use of the American system of initiative and profit. They were no more free than the worker or the farmer. Even honest and progressive-minded men of wealth, aware of their obligation to their generation, could never know just where they fitted into this dynastic scheme of things.

It was natural and perhaps human that the privileged princes of these new economic dynasties, thirsting for power, reached out for control over Government itself. They created a new despotism and wrapped it in the robes of legal sanction. In its service new mercenaries sought to regiment the people, their labor, and their property. And as a result the average man once more confronts the problem that faced the Minute Man.

The hours men and women worked, the wages they received, the conditions of their labor—these had passed beyond the control of the people, and were imposed by this new industrial dictatorship. The savings of the average family,

Speech given by Franklin D. Roosevelt in 1936 *(continued)*

the capital of the small business man, the investments set aside for old age—other people's money—these were tools which the new economic royalty used to dig itself in.

Those who tilled the soil no longer reaped the rewards which were their right. The small measure of their gains was decreed by men in distant cities.

Throughout the Nation, opportunity was limited by monopoly. Individual initiative was crushed in the cogs of a great machine. The field open for free business was more and more restricted. Private enterprise, indeed, became too private. It became privileged enterprise, not free enterprise.

An old English judge once said: "Necessitous men are not free men." Liberty requires opportunity to make a living—a living decent according to the standard of the time, a living which gives man not only enough to live by, but something to live for.

For too many of us the political equality we once had won was meaningless in the face of economic inequality. A small group had concentrated into their own hands an almost complete control over other people's property, other people's money, other people's labor—other people's lives. For too many of us life was no longer free; liberty no longer real; men could no longer follow the pursuit of happiness.

Against economic tyranny such as this, the American citizen could appeal only to the organized power of Government. The collapse of 1929 showed up the despotism for what it was. The election of 1932 was the people's mandate to end it. Under that mandate it is being ended.

The royalists of the economic order have conceded that political freedom was the business of the Government, but they have maintained that economic slavery was nobody's

Speech given by Franklin D. Roosevelt in 1936 *(continued)*

business. They granted that the Government could protect the citizen in his right to vote, but they denied that the Government could do anything to protect the citizen in his right to work and his right to live.

Today we stand committed to the proposition that freedom is no half-and-half affair. If the average citizen is guaranteed equal opportunity in the polling place, he must have equal opportunity in the market place.

These economic royalists complain that we seek to overthrow the institutions of America. What they really complain of is that we seek to take away their power. Our allegiance to American institutions requires the overthrow of this kind of power. In vain they seek to hide behind the Flag and the Constitution. In their blindness they forget what the Flag and the Constitution stand for. Now, as always, they stand for democracy, not tyranny; for freedom, not subjection; and against a dictatorship by mob rule and the over-privileged alike.

The brave and clear platform adopted by this Convention, to which I heartily subscribe, sets forth that Government in a modern civilization has certain inescapable obligations to its citizens, among which are protection of the family and the home, the establishment of a democracy of opportunity, and aid to those overtaken by disaster.

But the resolute enemy within our gates is ever ready to beat down our words unless in greater courage we will fight for them.

For more than three years we have fought for them. This Convention, in every word and deed, has pledged that that fight will go on.

The defeats and victories of these years have given to us as a people a new understanding of our Government and

Speech given by Franklin D. Roosevelt in 1936 *(continued)*

of ourselves. Never since the early days of the New England town meeting have the affairs of Government been so widely discussed and so clearly appreciated. It has been brought home to us that the only effective guide for the safety of this most worldly of worlds, the greatest guide of all, is moral principle.

We do not see faith, hope and charity as unattainable ideals, but we use them as stout supports of a Nation fighting the fight for freedom in a modern civilization.

Faith—in the soundness of democracy in the midst of dictatorships.

Hope—renewed because we know so well the progress we have made.

Charity—in the true spirit of that grand old word. For charity literally translated from the original means love, the love that understands, that does not merely share the wealth of the giver, but in true sympathy and wisdom helps men to help themselves.

We seek not merely to make Government a mechanical implement, but to give it the vibrant personal character that is the very embodiment of human charity.

We are poor indeed if this Nation cannot afford to lift from every recess of American life the dread fear of the unemployed that they are not needed in the world. We cannot afford to accumulate a deficit in the books of human fortitude.

In the place of the palace of privilege we seek to build a temple out of faith and hope and charity.

It is a sobering thing, my friends, to be a servant of this great cause. We try in our daily work to remember that the cause belongs not to us, but to the people. The standard is not in the hands of you and me alone. It is carried by America.

Speech given by Franklin D. Roosevelt in 1936 *(continued)*

We seek daily to profit from experience, to learn to do better as our task proceeds.

Governments can err, Presidents do make mistakes, but the immortal Dante tells us that divine justice weighs the sins of the cold-blooded and the sins of the warm-hearted in different scales.

Better the occasional faults of a Government that lives in a spirit of charity than the consistent omissions of a Government frozen in the ice of its own indifference.

There is a mysterious cycle in human events. To some generations much is given. Of other generations much is expected. This generation of Americans has a rendezvous with destiny.

In this world of ours in other lands, there are some people, who, in times past, have lived and fought for freedom, and seem to have grown too weary to carry on the fight. They have sold their heritage of freedom for the illusion of a living. They have yielded their democracy.

I believe in my heart that only our success can stir their ancient hope. They begin to know that here in America we are waging a great and successful war.* It is not alone a war against want and destitution and economic demoralization. It is more than that; it is a war for the survival of democracy. We are fighting to save a great and precious form of government for ourselves and for the world.

I accept the commission you have tendered me. I join with you. I am enlisted for the duration of the war.

---

* The "war" FDR speaks of here was not World War II but his war against the disastrous conservative economic policies that had plunged the nation into the Great Depression.

PART III

Governing for We the People

Americans stand at a critical moment in history. Do we follow the Founders and say that we want a government of, by, and for We the People, or do we follow the cons and choose a government of, by, and for inherited wealth and the elite of a corporatocracy?

We don't need to speculate about the outcome of either choice for the middle class. History, past and present, offers a clear answer.

Compare the stories of two presidents. Both went to war against what they called an "evil empire." Both won the military battle—at least enough to declare victory. Both were then faced with an enemy whose country was completely ruined. Both promised to help the people in that country pick up the pieces and rebuild their societies.

President A chose to give money directly to the foreign country's government on the theory that when you give money to We the People, they will make good decisions about how to spend it. President B chose to give money to big business on the theory that when you give money to the corporatocracy, it will make the best decisions about how to use it efficiently. Which president made the right choice?

President A was Harry S. Truman, who created the Marshall
Plan for Europe and helped rebuild Japan after World War II.
President B is George W. Bush, who is busily privatizing Iraq.

PRIVATIZING IRAQ

When George W. Bush started bombing Iraq, he told the world
that his undeclared war, Operation Iraqi Freedom (originally
named Operation Iraqi Liberation until a reporter noticed the un-
fortunate acronym), was going to be waged as much for the Iraqi
people as against Saddam Hussein.

In announcing a rather premature victory on the battleship
USS *Lincoln* in April 2003, Bush said:

> We're helping to rebuild Iraq, where the dictator built palaces
> for himself, instead of hospitals and schools. And we will stand
> with the new leaders of Iraq as they establish a government of,
> by, and for the Iraqi people. The transition from dictatorship to
> democracy will take time, but it is worth every effort. Our coali-
> tion will stay until our work is done. Then we will leave, and we
> will leave behind a free Iraq.

What Bush proposed was his own version of a Marshall Plan,
named after Truman's secretary of state, George Marshall. The
original Marshall Plan gave money to the governments of all the
European countries affected by World War II so that they could
import necessary materials and rebuild their country's industries.
(The Soviet Union forbade the countries under its control from
taking any of the $6 billion in funds allocated, so the rebuilding in
Europe was limited to the western countries.)

One of Truman's aims in creating the Marshall Plan was to
prove how important government is in creating a middle class.
He had had trouble passing reforms that would help the middle
class in the United States. In 1947, for example, congressional
Republicans shot down Truman's proposal for a national single-
payer health-care plan that would cover every American, and they

weakened union protections by passing—over Truman's unsuccessful veto—the Taft-Hartley Act. In part to show Americans that national health care and a strongly unionized workforce would help build a strong middle class, Truman encouraged Germany and Japan to incorporate these concepts into their new constitutions. Both did, and the results were impressive.

With the Iraq war, however, the cons saw an opportunity to prove Truman—and his embrace of government—wrong. They'd take a country with a protected economy, a strong public sector, high taxes on business, and national health care and turn it into a con's paradise.

In 2003, L. Paul Bremer III, then the head of the Coalition Provisional Authority, the U.S. de facto government of Iraq, issued Order 37, which dropped Iraq's corporate income tax from more than 40 percent to a 15 percent flat tax. His Order 39 allowed multinational corporations to enter Iraq, buy up formerly Iraqi companies, fire all their Iraqi employees if they chose, and even take 100 percent of their profits out of the country. He fired a half million public employees, including teachers, doctors, and nurses, to pave the way for complete privatization of the education and health-care sectors. He approved a law banning unions and outlawing collective bargaining in most business sectors. As Naomi Klein noted in an article for *Harper's*, Bremer said: "Getting inefficient state enterprises into private hands is essential for Iraq's economic recovery."[1]

The foundational con theory is that selfishness is the fundamental human urge, that the greed arising from it will motivate people to go into business, and that those businesses will then—to maximize their profits—meet all the needs of the people. With all human needs thus met, there is no need for government, other than perhaps to operate an army and a police department.

So instead of giving Iraqis money or loans so that they could rebuild their own country, Bush instead gave the money to Halliburton, Bechtel, Fluor, and a few other large, politically

connected multinational corporations. He rewrote the Iraqi constitution (in violation of international law) to turn Iraq into the
world's largest free-trade zone. He nearly perfectly followed the
script of the World Bank and other conservative corporatist institutions, administering "shock therapy" to the Iraqi economy. Iraq
was, the cons believed, the perfect opportunity to prove the cons'
belief that the corporatocracy will provide for the common good
and outshine Harry Truman's "liberal Democratic" successes in
Germany, Japan, and the rest of western Europe.

So, how well has privatization gone in Iraq? Almost three
years after Bush's undeclared war began, an article by the *Observer*
tells the story:

> More than a quarter of total US funds have been swallowed up
> by security, and in many parts of the country, even the most
> basic facilities are still missing. "Government is not functioning
> in so many sectors," says Oliver Burch of Christian Aid, which
> has several partner organisations working across Iraq.
>
> "The health budget for last year was $1 billion, but out in the
> provinces, doctors in hospitals and clinics are appealing to ev-
> eryone they can find, because they can't get the place painted;
> they can't get the toilet fixed; they can't get basic drugs." He said
> his partner-organisations feared corruption was partly to blame.
> "We think it's horrendously large in scale."

The story continues.

> Another problem is the gradual withdrawal of food aid. More
> than half of the families in Iraq still receive a monthly food
> parcel of basic supplies. Oliver Burch says this legacy of the oil-
> for-food programme in the long years of sanctions is expensive,
> and distorts the market. "Farmers aren't growing wheat, because
> there's no market for it," he says.[2]

In fact, Iraq's infrastructure appears to be in a worse condi-
tion than it was before the war. For example, the electricity supply
is still around 4,000 megawatts, about the prewar level. On average

there is twelve hours of supply a day. Meanwhile oil production is 1.1 million barrels a day, below prewar levels.

The *Guardian* tells us that the actual cost to the American people of the war in Iraq is going to top $2 *trillion*.[3] And yet the Iraqi people still experience severe shortages of food, electricity, and health care.

And it's not just the Iraqi people who've gotten screwed. The American taxpayers have footed most of the bill for this failed con demonstration project.

For example, from January 2004 to December 2005, Bechtel earned $1.8 billion in Iraq for assessing and repairing selected power, municipal water, and sewage systems; dredging, repairing, and upgrading the Port of Umm Qasr; rehabilitating selected schools, clinics, and fire stations; reconstructing three key bridges; constructing a key rail line; restoring telephone service to more than two hundred thousand Baghdad subscribers; and restoring Iraq's main 2,000-kilometer, north-south fiber-optic communications backbone. And yet Iraqis still have unreliable phone service and insufficient clinics.

Fluor Corporation, along with partner AMEC, won a $1.1 billion contract to repair Iraqi water systems in 2003 and has since won further contracts to repair electrical systems. Yet the electrical systems in Iraq are still worse than they were under Saddam.

But the big winner was Vice President Dick Cheney's former company, Halliburton, which has earned $13.6 billion in revenue for providing security to American troops and Iraqi oil installations; its stock price has tripled since the war began, from $20 to $63 per share.

Bush's war in Iraq was a huge success for corporate America. It redistributed wealth from American taxpayers to multinational corporations at an astonishing pace while leaving the Iraqi people literally in the dark.

But as a demonstration project proving that Truman's Marshall Plan was either wrong or a fluke, Iraq has failed the cons.

True believers to the end, though, they now say they're going do the same to America. They assure us that once public assistance for health care is privatized (by doing away with Medicare and Medicaid), Social Security is privatized, the unions are finally put out of business, public schools are privatized, and religion is funded by the government to take care of any remaining social needs (Bush gave churches more than $1.4 billion by executive order without an act of Congress during election year 2004), everything, they say, will become a paradise.

Sure, and that's why things are going so well in New Orleans, where the cons have given almost all of the $18 billion allocated so far in reconstruction money to the same big corporations that benefited in Iraq: Halliburton, Bechtel, and Fluor. After one year all that was fixed in New Orleans was the tourist business—which means big dollars for the hotel conglomerates. Most New Orleanans were still homeless, and most small businesses were still down. As in Iraq the dollars that poured into New Orleans are part of the biggest redistribution of wealth in our country's history, a redistribution from taxpayers to the corporate elite.

Every time such a social and economic structure has been tried in the past, it's led to the hellish world Charles Dickens characterized so well in his many books. And as we head into the third decade of the cons' economic and trade policies being imposed on America, it's becoming increasingly clear that all their talk about domestic privatization plans amounts to little more than an undeclared war on the middle class.

WHAT WE CAN DO

We don't have to sit back and allow the cons to take over. We have a model that works. It's the model Harry Truman used in Europe and Franklin Roosevelt used here to create the Golden Age of the middle class. It's based on the principles the Founders used to create democracy in this country.

Government must be of, by and for We the People. That means government institutions like the military, the prisons, and the electoral process must be publicly controlled, not in the hands of corporations or wealthy individuals. In a democracy We the People must be informed enough to make decisions about our society, which means that education in particular must be both free and public.

Democracy requires that government work for We the People. Its primary function is to define the rules of the game of business in a way that protects working people and allows a middle class to emerge. This includes regulating large predatory companies so that entrepreneurs can survive, providing a strong social safety net and national health care to make us competitive with other nations offering their citizens the same (and because it's necessary for a middle class), and protecting domestic industries (and jobs) by instituting tariffs—import taxes—on goods coming in from cheap-labor countries.

Finally, instead of the cons' "trickle-down" program, we need to return to a commonsense, classical economy that makes sure the people have a solid middle-class income and that trusts the people to spend it wisely. That means we need progressive taxation, pro-labor policies, and a living wage.

Iraqis faced one of the cons' undeclared wars and lost. The American middle class is facing another undeclared war. We can do something about it.

CHAPTER 9

Too Important for the Private Sector

Some aspects of government are just too important to hand over to the private sector.

Among these are the government's role in protecting life and liberty. Even the cons will say that the government has a role in defending citizens. But they just can't seem to help themselves. Since Ronald Reagan, the cons have been busy privatizing the most basic features of our government, including the military, the prisons, and our electoral system itself.

The cons ascribe to a religion of privatization. "Anything government can do, we can do better," they say. Even though corporations have to skim money off the top to pay dividends to their shareholders, pay their CEOs' huge salaries, and pay for the corporate jets, fancy headquarters, golden bathroom fixtures, and advertising and marketing, somehow the cons think corporations can do things more efficiently than a government that has to pay only civil servants. It defies logic, but they keep repeating this fundamental article of faith-based economics.

PRIVATIZING THE MILITARY

The second-largest army in Iraq is not the United Kingdom's but the thirty thousand or so private contractors hired by the Bush administration.

Corporations are now providing services that the army used to do. The cons tell us that private corporations are much more efficient than the army at providing services. Yet these corporations bring people over from the United States and pay them more than $100,000 a year, whereas the army starts privates at $15,282.[1] It doesn't make any sense economically.

Nor is using contractors more efficient in terms of getting the job done better and faster. In the foregoing introduction to part III, we saw that corporations have failed miserably at doing their jobs in Iraq. And it apparently takes more of them to *not* do those jobs. From 1999 to 2002, the U.S. government eliminated 48,000 civil service jobs while adding 730,000 contract positions.[2]

Privatizing the military is just another way for the cons to transfer hundreds of billions of tax dollars from We the People to the corporatocracy.

Because the army can't actually command private contractors, there's no real accountability. According to Michael Scherer, who wrote on this topic for *Mother Jones,* "A report the GAO [Government Accounting Office] released said a number of the weapon systems the U.S. has deployed need contractors to maintain them. Generals have no idea which jobs are being done by contractors. If the contractors walk off the job, that would hamper the military effort. There's no accountability."[3]

The Bush administration has even given up trying to make these corporations accountable to the government. Scherer points out that the government has shifted oversight of the work that private contractors do to the private contractors themselves. For example, Scherer reports,

> The U.S. government has its own agency that buys oil for the U.S. military called the Defense Energy Appropriation Center. But the Pentagon didn't give the contract to import oil for Iraq to that agency. They gave it to Halliburton. When you ask them why they gave the contract to Halliburton, they say, "Well,

Halliburton drew up the energy plans for us." Halliburton designed the contract they awarded to themselves.[4]

This lack of accountability doesn't just affect the financial cost of using private contractors for military work. There's a cost to democracy as well.

As anybody who's been in the military can tell you, the old cliché is true that the job of an army is to "blow things up and kill people." The nature of an army includes licensing people to kill other people. This license to kill is governed by national laws and by international treaties.

Private corporations, however, are under few such constraints when they act as a mercenary army on behalf of a government. While the government pays the corporation, the same laws and treaties do not govern it as they would an army of the government. A private corporation is not answerable to We the People. To the contrary, laws and Supreme Court precedents say that private corporations can hide things behind the secrecy of "corporate personhood," claiming Fourth, Fifth, and Fourteenth Amendment "human rights" in ways that governments never could.

When you combine that lack of oversight with the profit motive, you get situations like the horrendous torture at Abu Ghraib, a process that, according to people who were there, was heavily influenced by the presence of and the orders from "private contractors." At least a thirty-strong team of interrogators at the prison, for example, were employed by CACI International, which is based in Virginia.[5] According to the grunts who were convicted, private contractors told them to come in and do many of the things for which they went to jail: private contractors were in charge of many of the interrogations.

And there's nothing we can do about that. As Human Rights Watch notes, "These contractors operate in Iraq with virtual impunity—exempt by the terms of their engagement with the U.S. military from prosecution by Iraqi courts, outside the military chain of command and thus ineligible for court-martial, and not subject to prosecution by U.S. courts."[6] They act outside the law. If you are going to give someone the legal power to kill, you want those people to be under the absolute control of We the People.

PRIVATIZING PRISONS

Si Kahn and Elizabeth Minnich, authors of *The Fox in the Henhouse*, say that we are witnessing "a second American revolution, by the corporations, who are trying to upset the balance of power that has served us so well. We are talking about government by, of, and for the corporation."[7]

The privatization of America is especially pernicious when it comes to prisons. Most people don't know that there are prisons for profit. Anyone can build a prison without government authority. In *Lockdown America*, Christian Parenti tells us that corporate jailers now control roughly a hundred thousand prison beds nationwide in over a hundred different facilities in twenty-seven states.[8]

And that's a real problem for American liberty. As Kahn and Minnich explain, "If prisons are motels with bars, then from the corporate perspective making money is all about filling beds and providing food service. So corporations lobby aggressively to get as many people as possible locked up."

There are two insidious consequences of the privatization of our prisons. The first is that the quality of treatment and rehabilitation—which should be the first goal of imprisonment in most cases—has declined.

There are some people—a very small number—whom we put in prison because we really and truly never want them to be a part of society again. The vast majority of incarcerated people, however, are put there as a way of saying, "Don't ever try that again!" Once these people serve their time, we hope they will have learned their lesson and we invite them to return to society.

The prison system must have an element of punishment to it—that being intrinsic to a person's being deprived of liberty—but it must also have an element of rehabilitation because these people will end up back in society among the rest of us. The first problem with privatization, however, is that the private prison industry does not have any financial incentive to rehabilitate prisoners. It's much easier and cheaper for private industry to warehouse people than to provide them with education, job training, and drug or alcohol treatment.

It's much cheaper for society, however, to pay for rehabilitation programs. A study by the RAND Corporation shows that every dollar spent on treatment instead of imprisonment saves $7 in state costs. That's because treatment is significantly more effective at reducing drug use than is jail or prison.[9]

It typically costs a minimum of $20,000 per year to keep someone in prison.[10] On the other hand, if someone is out in the workforce, even if they've got a low-paying job, not only do they not cost society anything but they are now paying taxes. They are contributing to society. Our goal as We the People should be to have as few people in prison as possible, not as many as possible.

The second, and even more dangerous, problem with the privatization of our prisons is that the private-prison industry has become one of the major lobbyists in Congress for harsher penalties for relatively insignificant crimes. For example, the "three strikes" law doesn't mainly catch murderers and rapists. It catches the guy who shoplifts three times at the corner store or is caught abusing drugs three times. Now he's imprisoned for life.

There's a long history of corporate interests lobbying for harsh marijuana laws (for example), ranging from the initial laws pushed by the cotton growers (who saw hemp as an economic threat) to more recent laws pushed by drug-testing companies and private-prison companies. They're lobbying for heavier and harsher penalties because that means more money for them. And they are succeeding. That's one of the reasons why the United

States has locked up more than 2 million people—more people in prison both in absolute numbers and on a per-capita basis than any other nation in the world. The cons will say that all these people should be in prison. Yet former governor Gary E. Johnson of New Mexico, a Republican, has pointed out that "in 1980, the federal government arrested a few hundred thousand people on drug charges; today we arrest 1.6 million people a year for drug offenses. Yet we still have a drug problem."[11]

Vince Besser, writing in *Mother Jones* magazine, tells us that "Nationwide, crime rates today are comparable to those of the 1970s, but the incarceration rate is four times higher than it was then. It's not crime that has increased; it's punishment. More people are now arrested for minor offenses, more arrestees are prosecuted, and more of those convicted are given lengthy sentences."[12]

The simple fact is that when you privatize something, you create an incentive for that business to do more of what it does. If the business is warehousing people, that business will look for new customers. The way that the private-prison industry gets new customers is by encouraging lawmakers to criminalize more behaviors and by increasing the punishment for those behaviors already criminalized.

Van Jones, of the Ella Baker Center for Human Rights, points out:

> If what we want in urban America are peaceful streets and safe communities, the strategy we are pursuing is stupid. We are de-funding community programs and schools. We are de-funding what will keep kids out of trouble. We are funding prisons instead.

> It's been demonstrated statistically that every day a young person spends in prison, they are more likely to cause trouble when they get out. Prisons make our communities less safe. We all want community safety, but not a prison industry that is profiteering off making our community less safe.[13]

The first step in reducing crime is to take back our prisons from private industry. And we should work to reduce sentences when it is safe and reasonable to do so. With the money we save from warehousing people, we can pay for rehabilitation programs, turning people who deplete the community's resources into contributing members of society.

PRIVATIZING ELECTIONS

The ultimate crime of privatization is the privatization of our vote. In 2004 more than 80 percent of the U.S. vote was counted by three private corporations: Diebold, ES&S, and Sequoia.[14]

At the founding of this nation, we decided that there were important places to invest our tax dollars: in things that had to do with the overall "life, liberty and pursuit of happiness" of us all. Over time these commons—in which we all make tax investments and for which we all hold ultimate responsibility—have come to include our police and fire services, our military and defense, our roads and skyways, our food and drug supply, and our air, water, and national parks. But the most important of all the commons in which we've invested our hard-earned tax dollars is our government itself. It's owned by us, run by us (through our elected representatives), answerable to us, and most directly responsible for the stewardship of our commons.

And the commons through which we regulate the commons of our government is our vote.

That commons of our vote is now in danger. We have already seen several instances in which private control over voting may have been used to influence an election—or at least created the appearance of such influence.

Before stepping down and running for the U.S. Senate, Chuck Hagel (now senator from Nebraska) had been the chairman of the board of AIS, the owner of ES&S, a voting-machine company that had just computerized Nebraska's vote.[15] In 1997 the *Washington Post* said that Hagel's "Senate victory against an incumbent Democratic governor was the major Republican upset in the November election."[16] According to Bev Harris, author of *Black Box Voting*, Hagel won virtually every demographic group, including many largely black communities that had never before voted Republican.[17] Hagel was the first Republican in twenty-four years to win a Senate seat in Nebraska, nearly all on unauditable machines he had just sold to the state.

In Georgia—a state that went all-electronic just in time for the 2002 elections—the defeat of Democrat Senator Max Cleland raised eyebrows. On November 2, 3003, the *Atlanta Journal-Constitution* reported that "Cleland leads [Republican Rep. Saxby] Chambliss 49 percent to 44 percent among likely voters."[18] Cox News Service, based in Atlanta, reported just after the election that "pollsters may have goofed" because "Republican Rep. Saxby Chambliss defeated incumbent Democratic Sen. Max Cleland by a margin of 53 to 46 percent."[19] The Hotline, a political news service, recalled a series of polls Wednesday showing that Chambliss had been ahead in none of them. Nearly every vote in the state was made on an electronic machine with no audit trail.

After these and similar stories, Congressman Rush Holt of New Jersey introduced a bill into Congress requiring that a voter-verified paper ballot be produced by all electronic voting machines, co-sponsored by a majority of the members of the House of Representatives. Republican leaders Dennis Hastert and Tom DeLay successfully fought to keep it from coming to a vote, thus ensuring that there could be no possible audit of the votes of the 2004 electorate.

The rallying cry of the emerging "honest vote" movement must become: *Get corporations out of our vote!*

Why have we let corporations into our polling places, locations so sacred to democracy that in many states even international election monitors and reporters are banned? Why are we allowing corporations to exclusively handle our vote—and in a secret and totally invisible way? One such private corporation was founded by a family that believes the Bible should replace the Constitution, another is run by one of Ohio's top Republicans, and yet another is partly owned by Saudi and Venezuelan investors.

Of all the violations of the commons—all of the crimes against We the People and against democracy in our great and historic republic—this is the greatest. Our vote is too important to outsource to private corporations.

It's time that the USA—like most of the rest of the world—returns to paper ballots, counted by hand by civil servants (our employees) under the watchful eyes of the party faithful—even if it takes two weeks to count the vote and we have to go, until then, with the exit polls of the news agencies. It worked just fine for nearly two hundred years in the USA, and it can work again.

When I lived in Germany, they took the vote in the same way most of the world does—people fill in hand-marked ballots, which are hand-counted by civil servants taking a week off from their regular jobs, watched over by volunteer representatives of the political parties. It's totally clean and easily audited. And even though it takes a few days to completely count the vote (and costs nothing more than a bit of overtime pay for civil servants), the German people know the election results the night the polls close because the news media's exit polls, for two generations, have never been more than a tenth of a percent off.

We could have saved billions of dollars that have instead been handed over to Diebold, ES&S, and other private corporations.

If we must have machines, let's have them owned by local governments, maintained and programmed by civil servants answerable to We the People, using open-source code and disconnected from modems, that produce a voter-verified printed ballot, with all results published on a precinct-by-precinct basis, and with random audits mandated.

As Thomas Paine wrote at this nation's founding, "The right of voting for representatives is the primary right by which all other rights are protected. To take away this right is to reduce a man to slavery."

Only when We the People reclaim the commons of our vote can we again be confident in the integrity of our electoral process in the world's oldest and most powerful democratic republic.

CHAPTER 10

Knowledge
Is Power

One of the primary elements of a true, functioning, representative democratic republic, like we aim for here in the United States, is that its citizens be well informed.

When Thomas Jefferson wrote a letter to his friend J. Correa de Serra on January 28, 1786, and said, "Our liberty depends upon the freedom of the press and that cannot be limited without being lost," he was assuming that Americans knew how to read their daily newspapers.

Not anymore. A 2005 study by the National Center for Education Statistics revealed that about 5 percent of the adults in the United States are not literate in English, meaning 11 million people lack the skills to handle many everyday tasks. Some 30 million adults, or 14 percent of the population, have "below basic" skills in prose. Their ability is so limited that they may not be able to make sense of a simple pamphlet, for example. Another 95 million adults, or 44 percent of the population, have intermediate prose skills, meaning they can do only moderately challenging activities. An example would be consulting a reference book to determine which foods contain a certain vitamin.[1]

The cons' solution, as usual, is to privatize education. They say the public school system is too broken to fix. And just to make sure it stays broken, they passed the No Child Left Behind Act

(NCLB), which will cost the states more in property taxes and other taxes than they are going to get out of it.

The solution is not to go in with a hammer and destroy the schools. It is not to privatize the schools. It's to change the way we are teaching.

EDUCATION IS AN INVESTMENT

There is a growing consensus that something is melting down in our schools, but the solution is not to abolish free public education. The solution is to make free public education better.

All the issues around education come down to one question: investment or expense? The conservatives would have you think that any kind of social programs are expenses. It's really important to reframe the conversation in terms of investment.

We know that the investment in a preschool program like Head Start yields substantial returns down the road in terms of reduced crime, reduced expenses associated with the detention of people, and increases in the tax base. For every $1 you invest in Head Start, you get $9 back. The child is far healthier, less likely to end up in special education or the criminal justice system, and more likely to go to college. Preschool is an investment, not an expense.

The cons, however, don't get it. The whole con agenda seems to be, "Let's go back to a caste system." They are hearkening back to men like John Adams and Alexander Hamilton, who believed we should have a ruling class and a working class and that the ruling class should be literate and the working class should just know enough to make change when they buy something.

They are doing their best to destroy public education. They are trying to destroy the teachers' unions and starve the schools.

Traditionally, we've determined the success or failure of the U.S. public education system by how competent our citizens are at being part of the workforce, participating in our democracy, and having social mobility. Those are all things that you can measure, and in many ways they all relate back to building critical-thinking skills—seeing the big picture, being able to challenge conventional wisdom, thinking outside the box to use the old cliché—as much as they do to the actual imparting of information. We've historically seen education as an essential and organic part of our democracy and considered access to higher education—regardless of the parents' income level—to be one of the keys to building a strong middle class, a strong economy, and a strong nation.

The cons, however, see education as just another commodity. And if it's just a commodity, like shoes or carrots, there must be a simple way to measure it. So instead of measuring its impact on society, they say, "Let's just see how well our kids are doing at memorizing some of the things that we think are important."

THE WRONG MEASURE

The tragedy of treating education as a commodity is twofold. First, the things the cons are measuring in their one-size-fits-all tests don't include the basic issues of democracy, freedom, liberty, and the history of this nation.

Standardized tests don't let us know if our kids know the difference between the worldviews of Paine versus Burke or the differences in the vision of democracy between Plato and Jefferson. They don't test if our kids understand why the Boston Tea Party happened or what differentiated the Founders from the Royalists of 1776. And the tests the cons devise are not designed to teach kids a thing about the populist and progressive movements in the late-nineteenth and early-twentieth centuries, the Wobblies and the history of organized labor, or the history of Roosevelt's and Truman's battles with cons over programs like labor policy, national health insurance, and Social Security.

The second tragedy for us and our children is that the cons—in their effort to commodify education—have turned the testing over to a few large corporations. Back when I was in school in the 1950s and 1960s, our teachers would write up their own tests, sometimes even in longhand, and make copies of them on the mimeograph machine. The cost was just a few cents—basically the cost of the paper and the mimeo machine's amortization. But the testing companies can charge $5, $10, $20 or more for 5 cents worth of paper. And the No Child Left Behind Act requires schools to buy these tests from specific large, politically active testing companies.

Testing has gone from being insignificant—basically just IQ tests—during the Golden Age of the middle class to being a million-dollar-a-year industry in the Reagan eighties to a multi-billion-dollar annual industry after the passage of NCLB. They've used it as a way to privatize another part of education.

Combine that with the relentless pressure for school vouchers, the federal aid programs to religious schools, and the ongoing conservative assaults on every teachers' union contract that comes up for renewal and you get it that they want to destroy public education by completely privatizing it. The result will be that the rich won't see any difference (they're already sending their kids to private prep schools like Andover, where both George Bushes went), the poor will be left with a few token dregs of education, and the middle class will be squeezed even harder.

No Child Left Behind has really sped up this process. Once a school district accepts the federal money for NCLB, it has to agree to the federally mandated and corporate-run scoring system. And if your school fails the test twice in a row, you have to give kids the option of going to another school and then pay for their transportation. But there is no money budgeted to pay for that transportation. And every kid a school loses means fewer state and federal dollars for that school.

What school districts are finding is that they are getting screwed. The state of Utah, for example, one of the most conservative states in the Union, has refused to abide by the requirements of the law. And other states may soon follow.

The real problem with NCLB, however, is not that it is under-funded. The problem is the assumption that you can commodify education at all. You can't.

The No Child Left Behind Act, and other school-privatizing schemes, is really a blowback to a nineteenth-century "create kids for the factories" model of education. Teaching for the test is the worst thing you can do. Want to teach a child to hate learning? Drill them and you'll do that.

Different kids learn in different ways.[2] The most powerful thing a teacher can do is not to make sure that a child has memorized a test but rather to ignite in that child a passion for learning, a love of knowledge. It's to bring back their natural curiosity.

Children love to learn. In just their first few years, they learn a language, how to interact in a family, and a million details. Kids don't fail—schools fail. And part of that failure is the result of the cons' meddling with our schools in an effort to break them so that they can say, "See? We told you public education isn't any good. Now let's hand it over to the business sector." And then we're back to the old rigid caste system in which the only people who get a good education are the children of the wealthy and the corporate elite.

Education is not a consumer product. Schools are not a commercial activity. They are part of the commons and essential to a functioning democracy. We have an obligation to make education work because we are creating the future of our country in our schools.

CHAPTER 11

Medicine for Health, Not for Profit

Andy Stephenson was an activist, a vigilant worker on behalf of clean voting in America. He worked tirelessly to help uncover details of electronic voting fraud in the 2000, 2002, and 2004 elections. He devoted years of his life to making America a more democratic nation.

But in 2005 his friends had to pass the hat to help pay for surgery to save him from pancreatic cancer. The surgery cost about $50,000, but the hospital wanted $25,000 upfront, and Andy was uninsured.

We are the only developed democracy in the world where such a spectacle could take place.

Dickens wrote about such horrors in Victorian England—Bob Cratchit's son, Tiny Tim, in need of medical care that was unavailable without a wealthy patron like Ebenezer Scrooge—but the United Kingdom has since awakened and become civilized.

Even the tyrants of communist China provide health care to their people, a bitter irony for the unemployed American factory workers they've displaced and for the poorly insured Wal-Mart workers who sell their goods.

Through some serious online fundraising, we pulled together enough money to pay for Andy's surgery. Unfortunately, the delays in raising that much money meant that his cancer had advanced to the point where it killed him soon after the surgery. Andy Stephenson's story is something that could happen only in an oligarchic banana republic—or in the USA.

Rights versus Privileges

To understand what happened to Andy, we first have to look at the big picture. Is health care a right or a privilege? If it's a right, it's part of the commons. By being born into a society, you are entitled to health care. If it's a privilege, it makes sense that only the rich have full access to it and poor and uninsured working people may die from lack of coverage.

If you go back over the thousands of years of human history, you will discover that health care has always been considered a right. The village shaman was always available. People helped each other.

In this country, in the Golden Age of the middle class—from 1940 to 1980—most states had laws requiring that hospitals be nonprofit organizations and take in anybody who showed up on their doorstep. Most states had laws that required health insurance companies to be nonprofit. Blue Cross and Blue Shield, for example, began as nonprofit companies.

The thinking behind this was that we don't want someone making a profit off our health care—we want them making decisions based on what's best for our health.

All that changed starting in the 1980s, when Reagan, followed by Bush Sr., Clinton, and Bush Jr., began defining health care as a privilege, not a right. Public hospitals started being replaced by private hospitals. Nonprofit insurance was gradually replaced by for-profit insurance—now even many of the Blue Cross/Blue Shield programs are for-profit. People like Senate Majority Leader Bill Frist's father were able to acquire tremendous wealth—literally billions of dollars of personal riches—by privatizing the commons of health care and squeezing all the cash they could out of previously public hospitals.

Of the other thirty-six fully industrialized democracies in the world, every single one of them has concluded that health care is a right. The United States is the only country in which this debate, thanks to the cons, is still going on.

PRIVATE HEALTH CARE HAS FAILED THE MIDDLE CLASS

Although we now have the most expensive health-care system in the world, it has not succeeded in making the American people healthy.

► The United States ranks twenty-seventh in the world for the quality of its citizens' health.

► The United States has 45 million uninsured people.

► The United States ranks twenty-fifth in the world in life expectancy, infant mortality, and immunization rates.

Even our health insurance is often tragically deficient—about a quarter of all bankruptcies last year in this nation were among insured people who were wiped out by co-pays, deductibles, and not-covered hospital and health-care expenses. (And with the new 2005 bankruptcy law, such bankruptcies will be infinitely more difficult in the future for anybody who's not a millionaire.)

The cons say there are enough protections in place to help those who fall through the gaping holes in the health-care system. That's simply not true.

Fully insured people have died because their insurance companies refused to cover their treatment, calling it "experimental." Others couldn't get care because their insurance companies claimed their illnesses were "pre-existing conditions" and thus were not covered.

Increasingly, hospitals are turning away people or moving into a for-profit status that lets them avoid the obligation to serve people who can't pay. The bottom line is that health care is rationed in the United States, as the *Wall Street Journal* noted in a front-page article by Geeta Anand titled "The Big Secret in Health Care: Rationing Is Here."[1]

The article tells the story of Lorraine Micheletti, an intensive-care unit (ICU) nurse. "As her hospital faces a cost crunch," notes Anand, "she's under pressure to get patients out of the glass-walled unit quickly."

Laying it out in unsparing tones, the *Wall Street Journal* article notes: "The word for what Ms. Micheletti does every day in this 173-bed hospital is one of the big secrets of American health care: Rationing."

The article adds: "Sometimes, rationing causes Ms. Micheletti to take on her own hospital." But, overall, rationing at Northeastern Hospital has worked out well for its owners. "In 2002, it posted a profit of $2.6 million, on an operating budget of around $85 million." Still, it's tough. "While Ms. Micheletti has worked hard to decrease the average patient stay this year, one person can throw off her numbers. 'You can eat up all of your profits if one or two patients linger in the ICU,' she says."

And it's not limited to public hospitals. "Nursing homes also ration care," notes Anand's article. "They have little incentive to take very sick patients, because in many cases they receive a fixed reimbursement rate from insurance which doesn't cover the full cost of care. As a result, nursing homes often try to limit the number of severely ill patients they take, to make sure they can cover costs."

With our largely privatized health-care system, the rich get very good health care. But if you are uninsured and you are not in a crisis—if you have an early-stage symptom, say, of cancer, that could be diagnosed and treated—and you show up at a public hospital, odds are that you will not be diagnosed and not be treated. You will be turned away.

The cons say the solution is more competition. This is non-sense. Right now hospitals compete against each other, insurance companies compete against each other, doctors compete against each other, and we all get screwed. What we need is cooperation. When hospitals went private, they came under tremendous pressure to cut costs, and they did that by rationing and by laying off experienced nurses and replacing them with nurses' aides. Now nurses take care of eight or nine patients each. A ratio of 1 nurse to 4 patients in a medical/surgical clinic would provide better health care (and a ratio of 1:1 in the ICU). Cutting the nursing staff made a lot of money for the insurance companies and the private hospitals, made Bill Frist's father a billionaire, and made a lot of trouble for the rest of us.

When insurance companies went private, they too came under tremendous pressure to cut costs. They quickly noted that there's an easy way to do that: don't insure people who are likely to get sick. Insurance companies protect their profits by either refusing to insure people with "pre-existing conditions" or by charging them very high rates.

And they set the bar low. If you're self-employed and have tried to get private health insurance recently, you'll know that the companies send an adjustor to your house to screen you. They draw your blood and take your weight. If you weigh a few pounds over their "ideal," or they find any of your blood work a bit off, watch out—you may actually need health care, and therefore you'll pay higher rates, assuming they deign to cover you.

Meanwhile, because most of the system is private, We the People have no way to put a brake on costs. Pharmaceutical companies, for example, can charge as much as they want for their drugs because they know that cost is just passed on to the health insurance companies, who pass the cost on to us. That's why, even though Americans make up just 4 percent of the world's population, in 2004 we spent $4 trillion on health care. That's 40 percent of the money spent on health care on the entire planet for 4 percent of the world's population.

The problem isn't that American health care needs to be more competitive. The problem is that health care in America is treated as a privilege, and only the privileged have unfettered access to it.

HOW MUCH OF A RIGHT?

The solution to America's health-care problem is to join the rest of the first world and make health care a right for all citizens. The only question then becomes: How much of a right?

There are two ways to deliver health care in a society that considers health care a right.

One way is to create "socialized medicine" whereby the government provides all of the health care itself, largely through facilities that it owns and doctors and nurses whom it hires as federal employees. There may still be private hospitals or doctors for the very rich, but most of the hospitals in the country would be owned and run by the government, and the vast majority of health-care workers—from technicians to nurses to doctors—would be employees of the government. This is, by and large, the British system.

Another way is the "single-payer system," like they have in Germany. In this system the government is basically the insurance company. The very rich could still pay their own way if they want to be in separate high-end private hospitals (much like they fly in private jets instead of use the airlines), but most people would get their health insurance directly from the government. Hospitals and doctors would still be private—they would manage their own business and even compete with each other—but they would be paid, by and large, by the government's insurance program.

We already have both of these systems in the United States.

The Veterans' Administration is socialized medicine. The U.S. government owns all the VA hospitals and employs all the VA health-care workers. Veterans, just by showing their identification card, which proves they are veterans, can walk into any VA hospital or VA medical clinic and get care free of charge.

Our single-payer system is Medicare. Those Americans eligible for Medicare can mostly choose their own doctors and their own hospitals. They show their Medicare card to their health-care provider, who then bills the government.

Veterans tell me that they like the VA system, but there are also problems with it. When the government gets in a squeeze, it starts cutting back funding—until people get politically active. The problem is that veterans, while being a significant political group, aren't "all of us," so when they yell it's easier for politicians to ignore them than if everybody were yelling. Thus VA doctors, nurses, and other staff often feel underpaid and underequipped.

I experienced the single-payer system when I lived in Germany. What I liked most about it was that I was able to pick my doctor. I found a doctor who specialized in homeopathy as well as conventional medicine, and another one who specialized in herbology and conventional medicine. I could choose anybody anywhere, and all I had to do was show my health-care card—the equivalent of everyone's having fully funded Medicare.

The cons say that the only way to create a competitive market is privatization, but experience demonstrates that that's not true. Unregulated privatization tends to lead to monopoly because it is simply cheaper for a company to monopolize supply and then ration health care.

The best system is the one that allows We the People the most choice and still rewards diversity and innovation. The single-payer system does that by regulating the market but not regulating our choices within that market.

WE HAVE NATIONAL HEALTH
CARE ALREADY: MEDICARE

Ever since democratic president Harry Truman proposed a national, single-payer health insurance system, Republicans and "conservative" Democrats have fought it. Nonetheless, Lyndon Johnson did manage to slip a single-payer system through Congress in the form of Medicare.

Medicare terrifies the corporate cons because it has the potential—with a single stroke of legislation—to overnight become a program that covers every American, a national single-payer health insurance system.

This is one reason why Republicans inserted a poisoned pill into Medicare in 2005, creating a drug benefit but mandating that Medicare cannot negotiate wholesale prices with drug companies but must always pay full retail. The increased cost of this "benefit" will create a Medicare crisis.

The cons knew that if they allowed Medicare to negotiate for pharmaceuticals the way the Veterans' Administration does, Medicare and the Americans who depend on it would benefit, rather than the system's being weakened, which was their objective. Instead of creating a benefit that would actually make health care cheaper for millions of Americans and for the government, the cons created a "benefit" that's going to destroy Medicare.

Like the proposed privatization of Social Security, it's another attempt by the cons to further dismantle the safety net—and it's not forty years down the road but will come in this decade.

Medicare today is almost running in the red, and the "nonnegotiable" drug benefit will probably push it over that edge. Cons in the right-wing think tanks and in Congress are hoping that the upcoming Medicare crisis will provide a good excuse to then privatize it and kill it off.

We need to not only save Medicare but expand it to cover every man, woman, and child in America.

According to a study published in the *New England Journal of Medicine,* if all of America's health insurance companies, HMOs, and other middlemen were eliminated, and the government simply paid your medical costs directly to whomever you chose to provide you with health care, the savings would be so great that without increasing the health-care budget we could provide cradle-to-grave health care for every American.[2]

That's because for every $100 that passes through the hands of the government-administered Medicare programs, between $2 and $3 is spent on administration, leaving $97 to $98 to pay for medical services and drugs.

But of every $100 that flows through corporate insurance programs and HMOs, $10 to $34 sticks to corporate fingers along the way. After all, Medicare doesn't have lavish corporate headquarters, doesn't use corporate jets, and doesn't pay expensive lobbying firms in Washington to work on its behalf. It doesn't "donate" millions of dollars to politicians and their parties. It doesn't pay profits in the form of dividends to its shareholders. And it doesn't compensate its top executive with more than a million dollars a year, as do each of the largest of the American insurance companies.

Medicare has one primary mandate: serve the public. Private corporations also have one primary mandate: generate profit.

There are some things that government does do better than private for-profit industry, and providing affordable health care is a classic example, proven by the experience of every other nation in the industrialized world.

CHAPTER 12

The Truth about the Trust Fund

What do you do when you want to screw *only* the working people of your nation with the largest tax increase in history and hand those trillions of dollars to your wealthy campaign contributors yet not have anybody realize you've done it? If you're Ronald Reagan, you call in Alan Greenspan.

TAXING RETIREMENT

Through the Golden Age of the middle class—from 1940 to 1980—the top income tax rate for the superrich had been between 70 and 90 percent. Ronald Reagan wanted to cut that rate dramatically, to help out his political patrons. He did this with a massive tax cut in the summer of 1981.

The only problem was that when Reagan took his meat ax to our tax code, he produced mind-boggling budget deficits. Voodoo economics didn't work out as planned, and even after borrowing so much that this year we'll pay more than $100 billion just in interest on the money Reagan borrowed to make the economy look good in the 1980s, Reagan couldn't come up with the revenues he needed to run the government.

Coincidentally, the actuaries at the Social Security Administration were beginning to worry about the Baby Boomer generation, who would begin retiring in big numbers in fifty years or so. They were a "rabbit going through a python" bulge that would require a few trillion more dollars than Social Security could easily collect during the same twenty-year period of their retirement. We needed, the actuaries said, to tax more heavily those very persons who would eventually retire; so instead of using current workers' money to pay for the Boomer's Social Security payments in 2020, the Boomers themselves would prepay for their own retirement.

Reagan got Daniel Patrick Moynihan and Alan Greenspan together to form a commission on Social Security reform, along with a few other politicians and economists, and they recommended a near doubling of the Social Security tax on the then-working Boomers. That tax created—for the first time in history—a giant savings account that Social Security could use to pay for the Boomers' retirement.

This was a huge change.

Prior to this, Social Security had always paid for today's retirees with income from today's workers. The Boomers were the first generation that would pay Social Security taxes to both fund current retirees *and* prepay for their own retirement.

And after the Boomers retired and the savings account—called the Social Security Trust Fund—was spent, the rabbit would have finished its journey through the python and Social Security could go back to a pay-as-you-go taxing system.

Thus within the period of a few short years, Reagan dramatically dropped the income tax on America's most wealthy by more than half and roughly doubled the Social Security tax on people earning $30,000 or less. It was, simultaneously, the largest income tax cut in America's history (almost entirely for the very wealthy) and the most massive tax increase in the history of the nation (which exclusively hit working-class people).

"YOU CAN'T PAY BENEFITS WITH IOUS"

But Reagan still had a problem. His tax cuts for the wealthy—even when moderated by subsequent tax increases—weren't generating enough money to invest properly in America's infrastructure, schools, police and fire departments, and military. The country was facing bankruptcy.

No problem, suggested Greenspan. Just borrow from the Boomers' savings account—the money in the Social Security Trust Fund—and, because you're borrowing "government money" to fund "government expenditures," you don't have to list it as part of the deficit. Much of the deficit will magically seem to disappear, and nobody will know what you did until thirty years in the future when the Boomers begin to retire in 2015.

Reagan jumped at the opportunity, as did George H. W. Bush, as did Bill Clinton (although Al Gore argued strongly that Social Security funds should not be raided but instead put in a "lock box"). And so did George W. Bush.

The result is that all that money—trillions of dollars—that has been taxed out of working Boomers (the ceiling has risen from the tax's being on your first $30,000 of income to your first $90,000 today) has been borrowed and spent. Left behind are a form of IOUs—a unique form of Treasury debt instruments similar (but not identical) to the Treasury debt instruments our government normally uses to borrow money.

Paul O'Neill, former Bush Sr. Treasury secretary, recounts how Dick Cheney famously said, "Reagan proved deficits don't matter." Cheney was either ignorant or being disingenuous. It would be more accurate to say, "Reagan proved that deficits don't matter if you rip off the Social Security Trust Fund to pay for them and don't report that borrowing from the Boomers as part of the deficit."

As the Associated Press reported on April 6, 2005:

President Bush on Tuesday used a four-drawer filing cabinet stuffed with paper representing government IOUs the president said symbolized the Social Security Trust Fund's bleak outlook for meeting Americans' future retirement needs. . . .

"A lot of people in America think there is a trust—that we take your money in payroll taxes and then we hold it for you and then when you retire, we give it back to you," Bush said in a speech at the University of West Virginia at Parkersburg.

"But that's not the way it works," Bush said. "There is no trust 'fund'—just IOUs that I saw firsthand. . . .

"[Susan] Chapman [of the Office of Public Debt] opened the second drawer and pulled out a white notebook filled with pseudo Treasury securities—pieces of paper that offer physical evidence of $1.7 trillion in Treasury bonds that make up the trust fund."[1]

Later, Senator Rick Santorum made an odd admission for a Republican con: "You can't pay benefits with IOUs," he said on the Senate floor. "You have to pay it with cash."

And where will that cash—now nearly $2 trillion—come from over the next decades as Boomers begin to retire?

A Con-made Crisis

Technically (and legally) it's simple: the Social Security Trust Fund will give back its IOUs to the Treasury Department and in exchange for them get cash to pay the Boomers' retirement checks. Practically, though, it'll be a crisis of biblical proportions. For the Treasury to come up with that kind of cash will require either massive tax increases or increased massive borrowing—at a time when we're already borrowing so heavily that China is propping up our economy with weekly loans.

Thus, Bush talks about a "crisis" in Social Security with some accuracy. But he doesn't dare tell us what the real "crisis" is—or how Reagan and Greenspan set it up—because when it becomes widely known that Reagan set the course to steal the Boomers' Social Security savings, it will destroy the reputation of both supply-side economics and the Republican Party for generations to come. If the cons have their way, however, no one will ever know that they destroyed Social Security. That's because the cons—who have largely taken over the Republican Party—have figured out a way to convince young Americans to gut Social Security before the financial crisis begins.

Progressives make the mistake of thinking that today's Social Security debate is about Social Security. It's not. It's about creating single-party rule for a generation or more. To do that Republican cons believe that they need only to grab the hearts and minds of the generation currently under thirty—and they can do that, win or lose, by properly framing the Social Security debate.

According to exit poll data from the Associated Press, under-thirty voters were up more than 9 percent in voter participation in 2004, bringing 4.6 million new young people to the polls just since 2000.

And, as Martha Irvine of the Associated Press noted in an article in *USA Today* the week after the 2004 election, "This time, young voters were the only group that favored Democrat Kerry. The AP's exit polls found that under-30s favored Kerry over Bush, 55% to 44%."[2]

This was not lost on the Republicans. As Irvine noted in her article, even safe-seat Republican U.S. Senator Chuck Grassley of Iowa designed an entire ad campaign "targeting young people."

And many among this young demographic—the first generation in more than two hundred years raised in schools largely unable to teach civics and American history both because of budget cuts and fear of claims of "liberal bias" from conservative fanatics—are politically naive and ripe for the picking.

Those under thirty don't remember—or, largely, don't even know—that the leading causes of death among the elderly, the widowed, and the disabled after the stock market crash of 1929 included starvation and hypothermia. Before Franklin D. Roosevelt instituted Social Security in 1935, the majority of America's elderly lived in poverty. Today it's 11.9 percent, but take away Social Security and today's elderly poverty rate would be 47.6 percent.

These are statistics that the Republican cons and their corporate media will not be sharing with people under thirty.

Thus, as David King of Harvard's Institute of Politics told the AP's Irvine of the young vote: "I think that young people are there for the taking."

Joseph Stalin's year for the final consolidation of single-party rule in Russia was 1927, and that rule lasted more than fifty years. American cons are planning for a similar fifty-year horizon and intend to use "age warfare" as a tool to bring young people along.

Using Social Security to Divide and Conquer

Republican cons and their neurolinguistic-programming expert Frank Luntz had to figure out what issue could bring young people into the fold. Gay bashing was out, as young people are the most gay-tolerant of all demographic groups. Ditto for other "social" issues like abortion, the death penalty, and government posting of "Thou shall have no other gods before me" at taxpayer expense.

Similarly, young people weren't likely to easily fall for the cons' spin on "clear skies" efforts to increase pollution, phony "science" denying global climate change, "healthy forests" giveaways to timber company contributors, and "free-trade" policies that are hollowing out America's middle class. Cons may be able to spin these issues for the already "conservative" thirty–to–fifty-five "Reagan/Limbaugh demographic," but not for young people.

And elderly Democrats—who still clearly remember how Roosevelt's policies lifted America out of the Great Depression—are a group whose minds Republican cons won't change.

Republican strategists realized that the key to success would be to find an issue that would set the dying-off elderly Democrats against the rising numbers of voting-age youth. Social Security—which Republican cons have hated since its inception anyway—proved a perfect solution. All that Republicans had to do was claim that Social Security was a program designed to allow old Democrats to steal from the young.

So the tacticians at the Republican National Committee developed an elaborate sleight of hand. They'd use the Republican-manufactured Social Security "crisis" to convince young people of three fallacies:

► Republicans want young people to get the best "return on their Social Security tax dollar investment."

► Democrats don't care about the interests of young people but only want to pander to old people to get their votes.

► Selfish old people, their "special interest" lobby the American Association of Retired Persons (AARP), and the Democrats they "own" will prevent young people from getting the "benefits" of the "free" market.

Divide and conquer has been the Republican cons' slogan ever since Bush Sr. first used television advertising to mentally merge Michael Dukakis with a black killer, pitting whites against blacks in America. It worked then, and Republican cons are betting that pitting young people against the elderly will work just as magically now.

PRIVATIZING SOCIAL SECURITY

You can't just throw out Social Security, however. People like it too much. So what the Republicans have done is come up with an alternative to what they call "government socialism." Their solution to the Social Security crisis is—surprise—privatization. Turn over Americans' safety net to Wall Street, they say. "Private accounts" are the answer. Get government away from "your money." There they go again.

It's the same pattern we saw with the Federal Emergency Management Agency (FEMA) during the Katrina disaster and are watching in slow motion with Medicare. Si Kahn and Elizabeth Minnich have described it in their book, *The Fox in the Henhouse.* First break the system: get Social Security into so much debt that it looks like it can't be "fixed." Then blame the crisis on "big government" and offer private corporations as a model solution.

Specifically, the cons are suggesting that we take the current surplus in the Social Security Trust Fund—and, yes, there is a surplus at the moment—and "give it back to the people" in the form of private accounts, managed by private companies.

Private enterprise, not surprisingly, is more than willing to help out. Wall Street is salivating at the prospect of getting its hands on the trillions of dollars we've put into Social Security. Corporate cons can take fees, administrative costs, and transaction costs. They can churn accounts and make money with our money. They can make billions, and that's why they are spending millions on advertising and on lobbying con politicians on both sides of the aisle to get the message out.

The problem with this plan is that it will do nothing to enhance Social Security. It'll actually shorten the life of the trust fund because it would leave less money in the fund to provide benefits to future generations. And because the U.S. government has actually already borrowed that money, it would add more than a trillion dollars to our national debt in the first ten years.

THE TRUTH ABOUT SOCIAL SECURITY

The cons' suggestion that we privatize Social Security ignores a series of realities:

▶ Social Security is an anti-poverty insurance program, not an investment program. One-third of its payments don't even go to retirees but instead are distributed to—literally—widows, orphans, and people so disabled they can't work. (And people who outlive actuarial averages often get back more than they paid in.)

▶ Cons tell young people that they'll get "high returns" by investing their money in the stock market, and they have tables and charts to prove it. But the "high return" assumptions they're putting forward for private accounts assume that the U.S. economy will be growing so fast that there would be no need for any Social Security reform whatsoever.

▶ Even if Social Security does run low on cash in 2042 or 2052 (depending on which arm of Congress you're listening to), private accounts won't add a single penny to that cashflow problem. In fact, the borrowing necessary to fund the younger generation's private accounts will throw the system even further in the red.

The fact is that Social Security has helped more Americans than any other program in the nation's history. No matter how well our economy is doing, there are always people who simply cannot work: the old, the sick, the infirm, the disabled, and single mothers during their first year of motherhood. If this group doesn't have the means to support itself, the resulting pain is felt by all of society.

For this reason the Founders put into place the first welfare plans at the same time they were putting together the United States. As Thomas Jefferson noted in his 1787 *Notes on Virginia*,

> The poor who have neither property, friends, nor strength to labour, are boarded in the houses of good farmers, to whom a stipulated sum is annually paid. To those who are able to help themselves a little, or have friends from whom they derive some succours, inadequate however to their full maintenance,

supplementary aids are given, which enable them to live comfortably in their own houses, or in the houses of their friends.

When Roosevelt created the Social Security program as part of his New Deal for America's working people, he extended and expanded the social safety net first put in place by George Washington (over the objection of the cons of his day). It would be tragic if the cons are successful in destroying this most important part of the fabric of American life.

CHAPTER 13

Setting the Rules of the Game

One of the most pernicious claims the corporatocracy makes is that business flourishes best in a perfectly "free" market. And when business flourishes, they say, all of society does better. It's the old trickle-down philosophy that inevitably produces a nation of peons.

Always get suspicious when you see the words *free market.* Let's go back to the story of Mrs. Flores, whom you met in chapter 2—the woman who lost her job at Levi Strauss when that venerable American company closed all of its factories here in the USA and moved them overseas.

Cons argue that "productivity" is responsible for the loss of American jobs. They love to quote nineteenth-century economist David Ricardo (1772–1823) as saying in his 1817 work *On Wages,* "Labour, like all other things which are purchased and sold, and which may be increased or diminished in quantity, has its natural and its market price."

Thus, they say, it's natural that American wages should have been in a free fall ever since Bill Clinton signed NAFTA and GATT: America's roughly 100 million workers now have to compete "on a level playing field" with 5 billion impoverished people around the world. Offshoring is simply the normal extension, they say, of Ricardo's classic view of economics.

What they conveniently forget is that Ricardo didn't say the market price was the natural price. On the contrary, he wrote, "The natural price of labour is that price which is necessary to enable the labourers, one with another, to subsist and to perpetuate their race, without either increase or diminution."

In other words labor is part of the game of business, and one of the first goals of the game of business is to "perpetuate" the existence of the laborers themselves. That's the *natural* price. If businesses want to keep their workers, according to Ricardo, they must make sure that the *market* price of labor is at least as much as the natural price of labor. And the natural price is the "subsistence" price— just enough to survive—which brings us back to Dickens's world.

On the other hand, when in 1914 Henry Ford raised his workers' pay to $5 per day (about double what other manufacturers were paying), he said he was doing so in part because he wanted his employees to be able to buy his cars. If the American workforce can't make a decent living, they'll stop buying products made in America, which will lead to fewer people making a decent living—this death spiral for an economy and a nation's middle class that we are now seeing as a result of Reagan/Clinton/Bush trade and economic policies.

Everybody knows that games played without rules won't work. Boxers are divided into weight categories to ensure relative fairness in fights; baseball rules define the type of bats that can be used; football players are limited in how they can use their hands so they don't injure opponents or gain unfair advantage.

What's lost on many Americans is that business is a game, too. And We the People define its rules through our elected representatives. The goal of the game is to provide for the life, liberty, and pursuit of happiness of American citizens.

GAMING THE SYSTEM

If government can create conditions that cause a middle class to emerge, by implementing fair rules for business, progressive taxation, and free public education, the opposite is also true: government can create a corporatocracy by deregulating business, by cutting taxes on extreme wealth, and by privatizing as much of the commons as possible. Cons call this "starving the beast."

Here's how you starve the beast: you put through tax cuts for the rich, which cuts back the revenues of the federal government to the point that, if you got rid of all the social programs, you'd have a balanced budget. No more Social Security, no more spending for education, no more spending for Medicare and Medicaid; have the government simply keep the armies, prisons, and police. Let's shrink government—that's their philosophy.

When you cut all those social programs, you lose the middle class and in its place create a very small, very wealthy elite and a large underclass of starvation-wage workers. You lose democracy and instead create corporatocracy. You change the rules of the game; We the People lose, and the feudal lords win.

Cons have been winning this particular game of "starve the beast" since Reagan first started seriously playing it in 1981. They've done it in large part by lying to the American people; and they've had to do that because if they told the truth the majority of Americans would throw them out of office.

This is, after all, still a democracy. If the majority of us agree to get rid of Social Security so that only the wealthy can have retirement benefits and the old are left to fend for themselves, so be it. If a guy breaks his back and can't work and the majority of us decide not to help people who are disabled, and as a result he has to beg on the street, well, we can democratically decide to screw him and ourselves.

But the cons are not having this debate in an open and honest fashion. They are not asking We the People if we want to get rid of, for example, the Head Start program. They could ask, "Do we want to invest in our youth now or not?" We know that if we invest in educating the very young, fewer of them will become criminals. It will save us money over the long term. But if the majority of us say, "No, we would rather pay $50,000 to imprison them later than pay $300 to put them in Head Start now," then fine, it's a democracy. But that's not the way the cons are doing it.

Instead of explaining why it would be better for Americans to give all their money to a corporate elite, they're giving huge tax cuts to the rich while pretending that the tax cuts benefit all Americans.

Instead of arguing that Americans should not expect the right to health care or security in their old age, they are prompting a government crisis by handing to the rich money they're borrowing from China, Japan, and Korea in the name of our grandkids. We are borrowing so much money from these countries that if they so much as blink, our currency could crash.

And that's just what the most ideological of the con elite want. They want an economic crisis because they figure that's the only way they can force a cut in spending on social programs.

In 2004 they thought they had starved the beast enough and sent Bush out on the campaign trail to advocate getting rid of Social Security—privatizing it, putting it in the hands of Wall Street. But it didn't work. Turns out We the People apparently like Social Security. So the cons went back to starving the beast. Bush instead passed a new series of tax cuts, with more to follow.

The cons are trying to play the game so that the rich benefit while the rest of us lose out. They get tax cuts, and we get program cuts. That's not the "free" market. That's a market that's being created for the benefit of the rich at the expense of the middle class.

HOW THE GAME WORKS

The question Americans have faced since the first arguments between Thomas Jefferson and Alexander Hamilton in the 1780s was whether the game of business should be played with the primary goal of enriching the few, or—while allowing the few to enrich themselves—enhancing the quality of life of the many.

The cons suggest that if the rich win first, benefits will "trickle down" to the rest of us. Protecting workers, they say, will produce abnormalities and dislocations from the "free" market. For example, they suggest that when minimum wages are fixed by government, and labor can lawfully bargain to increase wages by increasing scarcity of labor through union actions, the result is an increase in prices, ultimately "hurting the working person."

But the economist they most often cite on this thinking, David Ricardo, disagreed that raising wages first increased prices. He noted, "On the contrary, a rise of wages, from the circumstance of the labourer being more liberally rewarded, or from a difficulty of procuring the necessaries on which wages are expended, does not, except in some instances, produce the effect of raising price, but has a great effect in lowering profits."

In other words, all the talk about keeping wages down to keep prices down is a smokescreen: business owners want to keep wages down to keep profits up.

And when wages go down, profits do indeed go up. American wages have been falling steadily since Reagan first reintroduced con economics in 1980, and American corporations are generally more profitable than they've been in decades. In part this is not only because wages are going down within the United States but also because U.S.-level wages are being replaced by India- and China-level wages through outsourcing and offshoring.

"But offshoring isn't the problem for American workers!" the cons shout. "It's the increase in productivity. American businesses need fewer workers because automation and hard work have made our workers more productive."

This is a tragic lie, and it's been bought hook, line, and sinker by most American politicians and even many economists.

Productivity is, very simply, the measure of how many products or services can be produced for how many dollars of labor expended. But offshoring distorts productivity figures in two ways.

First, foreign labor is cheaper, but it produces nearly identical amounts of product or service. The result is "increased productivity."

Second, many corporations don't list offshore labor on their balance sheets as a labor expense. Because they hire offshore companies as subcontractors to do work previously done by their own employees, they get to reduce the number and the cost of their employees while having an only slightly increased line item for the subcontractor on their profit-and-loss statements. The result implies that the remaining employees are getting more done because the offshore employees are no longer counted in the productivity figures.

But the Indians and the Chinese know something you won't hear on con "business" programs: while China and India eagerly let multinational corporations move work to their nations from the United States, they fiercely protect their own domestic industries primarily through the use of tariffs—taxes on imported goods—and the strict regulation of imported labor.

Winning the Game for America

To return balance to the international game of business, America should follow the lead of the Chinese and the Indians. We can use tariffs to balance trade relationships.

From the founding of this country, our operational principle was: If there's a dollar's worth of labor in a pair of shoes made here, and you can make the same shoes in some other "cheap labor" country with 10 cents' worth of labor, there will be a 90-cent import tax (tariff) when you bring them into the country, to protect our domestic industries and our manufacturing jobs. Tariffs level the field for both American business and American labor. Without tariffs the only winners are the East India Company's modern incarnations—the multinational corporations (which is why the multinationals push so hard for the WTO and other such institutions, treaties, and trade agreements).

This is not a new idea, by the way—it's how America has protected its economy from the founding of this nation right up until Clinton signed NAFTA and GATT. The first law imposing tariffs was in place before the Constitution was ratified in 1789. Tariffs represented 100 percent of federal government revenues from the founding of this nation until around the time of the Civil War and about a third of our total federal revenues up to World War I. They were still a major source of revenue right into the 1980s, when Reagan first took a whack at them.

For example, Jefferson wrote in his diary on March 11, 1792: "Hamilton had drawn [Jean Baptiste] Ternant into a conversation on the subject of the treaty of commerce recommended by the National Assembly of France to be negotiated with us." France wanted concessions from America as a way of enhancing international relations but was unwilling to reduce its own tariffs. Jefferson noted, "Hamilton communicated this to the President, who came into it, and proposed it to me. I disapproved of it, observing, that such a volunteer project would be binding on us, and not them; that it would enable them to find out how far we would go, and avail themselves of it."

George Washington was more of Hamilton's mind. "However," Jefferson wrote,

> the President thought it worth trying, and I acquiesced. I prepared a plan of treaty for exchanging the privileges of native subjects, and fixing all duties forever as they now stood. Hamilton

did not like this way of fixing the duties, because, he said, many articles here would bear to be raised, and therefore, he would prepare a tariff. He did so, raising duties for the French, from twenty-five to fifty per cent. So they were to give us the privileges of native subjects, and we, as a compensation, were to make them pay higher duties.

The deal ultimately fell through—Jefferson saw it as a Machiavellian scheme by Hamilton to try to irritate England—but it shows how tariffs were an important aspect of American foreign policy from the administration of George Washington up until Bill Clinton got us into the World Trade Organization, thus eliminating most tariffs and trade "restrictions," letting multinational corporations instead of sovereign nations write the rules of international business.

To solve the crisis of the disappearance of America's middle class, the United States should follow Jefferson's lead and protect American workers. We should pull out of the WTO, NAFTA, CAFTA, and other multilateral treaties that give corporations the power to enforce their will on our government and our workers. This will again allow us to impose leveling tariffs on work done overseas. Offshore labor can then be set in price—by adding tariffs to it—to equal a living wage in the United States.

If a company wants to hire people to answer the phone in India for $2 per hour, fine. Let them do it—and pay a $10-per-hour tariff on top of the $2 hourly wage. If somebody wants to manufacture a computer in China with $10 worth of labor that would be worth $100 in the United States, no problem—just impose a $90 tariff on it when it's imported. Most companies will simply return to the United States for their labor, and those that don't will enhance government coffers with funds that can be used for national health care and the education of our workforce.

This is easily doable. By walking away from the Anti-ballistic Missile Treaty and the Kyoto accords, George W. Bush showed

Americans that we really do have the power to simply ignore or disavow international treaties to which we've already committed. It's time to apply that experience to the WTO, GATT, and NAFTA and return to our Founders' ideal of a nation in which the rules of trade and business are, as Jefferson said, "very much guided" by the interests of We the People rather than by a handful of multinational corporations.

CHAPTER 14

The Illegal Employer Problem

Working Americans have always known how to create a middle class. It's a simple equation: more workers, lower wages; fewer workers, higher wages.

Today wages are low in America because there are too many workers. Facilitating a rapid increase in the workforce by encouraging companies to hire noncitizens is one of the three most potent tools conservatives since Ronald Reagan have used to convert the American middle class into the American working poor. (The other two are ending tariffs [chapter 13] and destroying government protections for unions [chapter 15]).

Do the math. According to the Bureau of Labor Statistics (BLS), there are more than 7 million unemployed Americans right now. Another 1.3 million Americans are no longer counted because they've become "long-term" or "discouraged" unemployed workers (the BLS calls them "marginally attached"). And although various groups have different ways of measuring, most agree that at least another 5 million to 10 million Americans are either working part-time when they want to work full-time or are "underemployed," doing jobs below their level of training, education, or experience. That's between 8 million and 20 million unemployed and underemployed Americans, many unable to find above-poverty-level work.

At the same time, there are between 7 million and 20 million working illegal immigrants diluting our labor pool.[1]

If illegal immigrants could no longer work, unions would flourish, the minimum wage would rise, and oligarchic nations to our south would have to confront and fix their corrupt ways.

The cons like to blame the immigrants. They call what's happening an "illegal immigration" problem. It's not. We don't have an illegal immigration problem in America. We have an illegal employer problem.

ILLEGAL WORKERS: THE CONS' SECRET WEAPON

As David Ricardo pointed out in his 1814 treatise *On Labor,* there is an "Iron Law of Labor": when labor markets are tight, wages go up. When labor markets are awash in workers willing to work at the bottom of the pay scale, unskilled and semiskilled wages will decrease to what Ricardo referred to as "subsistence" levels.

Two years later Ricardo pointed out in his *On Profits* that when the cost of labor goes down, the result usually isn't a decrease in product prices but an increase in corporate and CEO profits. This is because the marketplace sets prices but the cost of labor helps set profits. For example, when Nike began manufacturing shoes in third world countries with labor costs below those in the United States, it didn't lead to $15 Nikes; their price held—and even increased—because the market would bear it. Instead that reduction in labor costs led to Nike CEO Phil Knight becoming a multibillionaire.

Republicans understand this very, very well, although they never talk about it. Democrats seem not to have read Ricardo, although the average American gets it at a gut level.

In the 1980s Ronald Reagan got it. His amnesty program, combined with his aggressive war on organized labor, in effect told both employers and noncitizens that there would be few penalties and many rewards for increasing the U.S. labor pool with undocumented immigrants.

The fact is that before Reagan's crackdown on organized labor, illegal immigration was never a serious problem. Take Mexico as an example. Before Reagan's presidency, an estimated 1 million people annually came to the United States from Mexico,[2] and the same number, more or less, returned to Mexico at the end of the agricultural harvest season. Very few stayed because there were no jobs for them.

But Reagan put an end to that. One million people per year continued to cross our southern border, but they stopped returning home each fall because they were able to find permanent employment.

The magnet drawing them? Illegal employers.

Between the start of the Reagan years and today, the private workforce in the United States has gone from being about 25 percent unionized to 7 percent, according to the Bureau of Labor Statistics. Much of this is the direct result—as César Chávez predicted—of illegal immigrants competing directly with unionized and legal labor. Although it's most obvious in the construction trades over the past thirty years, it's hit all sectors of our economy.

Cons of both parties appreciate the impact of illegal immigrants on the U.S. workforce. During the past campaign cycle, Democratic Party strategist Ann Lewis sent out a mass e-mail on behalf of a current Democratic senator, suggesting that the United States create "an earned path to citizenship for those already here, working hard, paying taxes, respecting the law, and willing to meet a high bar for becoming a citizen." Sounds nice. The same day on his radio program, Rush Limbaugh told a woman whose husband is an illegal immigrant that she had nothing to worry about with regard to deportation of him or their children because all he'd have to do, under the new law under consideration, is pay a small fine and learn English.

The directors of Wal-Mart are smiling.

Meanwhile the millions of American citizens who came to this nation as legal immigrants, who waited in line for years, who did the hard work to become citizens, are feeling insulted, humiliated, and conned.

The Cons' Twofer: Guest Workers

Cons can't just come out and say that they are pleased that the estimated 7 million to 20 million illegal workers in the United States are driving down wages. They can't admit that, behind oil revenue, Mexico's second-largest source of income is money sent home from illegal "cheap labor" workers in the United States. They won't acknowledge the corporate benefits of a workforce whose health care is paid for by U.S. taxpayers but whose productivity belongs to their corporate masters.

Instead, catering to compassionate Americans who don't realize that this is all about driving up corporate profits and driving down workers' wages, cons like Arlen Specter are promoting legislation that would decriminalize the illegals currently in the United States, thus making legal our increased workforce, while not giving those new workers the rights of citizenships—that's a twofer for the cons: workers who can't vote.

As Rachel L. Swarns reported in the *New York Times* on February 25, 2006: "Advocates for immigrants said the [Bush/Specter] plan failed to protect the rights of immigrant workers, who they argue deserve a clear path to citizenship. And the AFL-CIO warned that a guest worker program of unlimited scale would depress wages and working conditions while creating a perpetual underclass of foreign workers."

Shouldn't we invite people to become Americans and share in our great traditions of freedom and democracy? Of course.

Shouldn't we show compassion to those who suffer in countries where there is no strong middle class? Of course.

But there is nothing compassionate about driving down the wages of any nation's middle class.

There is nothing compassionate about being the national enabler of a dysfunctional oligarchy like Mexico. By sending an estimated $20 billion to Mexico every year,[3] illegal immigrants here are effectively supporting an anti-democratic, antiworker administration there that gleefully ships out of that nation its troublesome citizens—those lowest on the economic food chain and thus most likely to foster "labor unrest." Mexico and other "sending nations" need not deal with their own social and economic problems so long as U.S. employers are willing to solve them for them—at the expense of our middle class.

But what about repressive regimes? Aren't we denying entrance to this generation's equivalent of the Jews fleeing Germany?

This is the most tragic of all the arguments put forward by the cons in the hopes that compassionate progressives will bite. Our immigration policies already allow for refugees—and should be expanded. It's an issue that needs more national discussion and action. But giving a free pass to already corrupt oligarchies to send unwanted, troublesome workers to the United States—and equating this to the Holocaust—is an insult to the memory of those who died in Hitler's death camps and to those suffering in places like Darfur under truly repressive regimes. There is no equivalence.

Without a middle class, any democracy is doomed. And without labor having power in relative balance with capital/management—through control of labor availability—no middle class can emerge. America's early labor leaders did not die to increase the labor pool for the robber barons or the Walton family; they died fighting to give control of it to the workers of their era in the hopes that we would retain our labor power and inspire other nations with the same idea of democracy and a stable middle class.

CORPORATIST CONS AND RACIST CONS

Con strategists have noticed that the workers—the voters—of the United States are getting nervous about the fact that, according to the Pew Hispanic Center, "undocumented workers fill one out of every four agricultural jobs, 14 percent of construction jobs, and 12 percent of those who work in food preparation." This has led con commentators and politicians to resort to classic wedge-issue rhetoric, exploiting Americans' fears, while working to retain the status quo.

While corporatist cons quietly continue to talk about amnesty, racist cons worry out loud about brown-skinned Middle Eastern terrorists slipping in among the brown-skinned South and Central Americans. They even find themselves obligated—catering to both working-class fears and the bigots among us—to promote the idea of giant fences around the country to keep illegals out.

Lou Dobbs, the most visible media champion of this issue, always starts the discussion with a basic syllogism:

1. Our border is porous.

2. People are coming across our porous border and diluting our labor pool, driving down U.S. wages.

3. Therefore we must make the border less porous.

Lou's syllogism, however, ignores the real problem, the magnet drawing people to risk life and limb to illegally enter this country: illegal employers. The fact is that some 20 percent to 40 percent of all immigrants working here illegally didn't coyote across the border; they came here legally, with tourist or student visas, then simply stayed when their visas expired.[4] From 2000 to 2005, the greatest percentage increase in illegal immigrants didn't come from Mexico—it came from India and Brazil.[5] A border fence just doesn't make any sense.

Fifty years ago we didn't have an illegal immigration problem because we didn't have a conservative illegal employer problem. As the *Washington Post* noted in a June 2006 article:

> Between 1999 and 2003, work-site enforcement operations were scaled back 95 percent by the Immigration and Naturalization Service, which subsequently was merged into the Homeland Security Department. The number of employers prosecuted for unlawfully employing immigrants dropped from 182 in 1999 to four in 2003, and fines collected declined from $3.6 million to $212,000, according to federal statistics.
>
> In 1999, the United States initiated fines against 417 companies. In 2004, it issued fine notices to three.[6]

The hiring crimes of illegal employers are being ignored by the law and rewarded by the economic systems of the nation. Politically, this is not a civil rights issue, it's a jobs issue, as working Americans keep telling pollsters over and over again.

So long as progressives argue this issue on the basis of "illegal immigration," they'll lose—even when they're right. The cons, with their hysteric and racist talk of mass deportations and fences, will win. Instead of illegal immigration, progressives need to be talking about illegal employers.

WE DON'T NEED A FENCE

We don't need fences or posses to keep the American middle class healthy. All we need is for employers to follow the laws we currently have.

Start penalizing illegal employers, and noncitizens without a Social Security number will leave the country on their own. Tax law requires that an employer must verify the Social Security number of all employees to document, and thus deduct, the expense of their labor. This is a simple task, and some companies, such as AMC Theatres, are already doing it.

The *Washington Post* noted in a piece on April 30, 2006, that AMC, not wanting to be an illegal employer,

> has long submitted lists of its employees' Social Security numbers to the Social Security Administration [SSA] for review. If discrepancies arise, [Bell] said in an e-mailed response to questions, "we require the worker to provide their original Social Security card within 3 days or to immediately contact the local SSA office." She said the process is part of payroll tax verification and occurs after hiring.

Easy, simple, cheap, painless. No fence required. No mass deportations necessary. No need for Homeland Security to get involved.

The Republican (and Democrat) corporatists who want a cheap labor force and the Republican (and Democrat) racists who want to build a fence and punish humanitarian aid workers are equally corrupt and anti-progressive. So long as employers are willing and able to hire illegal workers, people will risk their lives to grab at the America Dream. When jobs are not available, most undocumented workers will simply leave the country (as they always have) or begin the normal process to obtain citizenship that millions (including my own sister-in-law—this hits many of us close to home) go through each year.

It's time to stop talking about "illegal immigration" and time to start talking about how the cons are trying to replace the American middle class with a labor pool of "working poor" Americans and powerless illegal (or "guest") immigrants—all so CEOs can fatten their wallets and further reward the conservative investor class.

Only when we start doing something about illegal employers will the countries to our south—and east and west—have an incentive to get their own economic houses in order, and only then will our middle class begin to recover the bargaining power and the living wages that are its due.

CHAPTER 15

Leveling the Playing Field

You can't be middle class if you earn the minimum wage in America today.

The American dream and the American reality have collided. In America we have always said that if you work hard and play by the rules, you can take care of yourself and your family. But the minimum wage is just $5.15 per hour. With a forty-hour workweek, that comes to a gross income of $9,888 per year. Nobody can support a family, own a home, buy health insurance, or retire decently on $9,888 per year!

What's more, 30 million Americans—one in four U.S. workers—make less than $9 per hour, or just $17,280 a year. That's not a living wage either.

The U.S. Census Bureau's statistics for 2004 show the official poverty rate at 12.7 percent of the population, which put the number of people officially living in poverty in the United States at 37 million. For a family of four, the poverty threshold was listed as $19,307.[1] If the head of that family of four were a single mother working full-time for the government-mandated minimum wage, she couldn't even rise above the government's own definition of poverty.

Becoming middle class in America today is like scaling a cliff. Most middle-class Americans are clinging to the edge with their fingernails, trying not to fall. In the 1950s middle-class families could live comfortably if just one parent worked. Today more than 60 percent of mothers with children under six are in the workforce.[2] Not only do both parents work but often at least one of those parents works two or more jobs.

MIDDLE CLASS AT EIGHTY HOURS PER WEEK

In a 2005 article in the *Chicago Tribune,* reporters Stephen Franklin and Barbara Rose introduce us to Muyiwa Jaiyeola.[3] Jaiyeola, who is thirty-three years old, works a forty-hour week as a salesman at a Sears store, then works another twenty hours in the stockroom of a Gap store in downtown Chicago. When Jaiyeola pulled two all-night shifts at his stockroom job in late August, he was able to sleep only two hours in the afternoon, then two more in the morning before going back to his sales job. He hoped to nap during his break in the middle of the night.

Jaiyeola is not hoping to get rich—he's just trying to pay his bills. Working two jobs at this wage level is what it takes to be middle class these days. And he's not alone. According to Franklin and Rose:

> Nearly 7.6 million Americans straddle two or more jobs and must find time to work, sleep and live somewhat contorted lives in a very full 24 hours. According to a 2001 U.S. Labor Department survey, most workplace moonlighters do it because they want or need extra money to pay bills. . . . Those who specifically need the extra work to pay bills are most often women who take care of their families, and divorced, widowed or separated workers.

For a quarter of the American workforce, not only is the American dream not a reality, no *part* of it is.

Low wages are being paid not only to entry-level workers at places like Wal-Mart and McDonald's but also to adults like Jaiyeola who have work experience. The people being forced to work two jobs to make a living are the heartbeat of our society.

They are child-care workers and nursing-home workers, janitors and security guards, salespeople and stockers. They often have the most hazardous jobs, the late-night jobs—the jobs that rarely include benefits.

Americans have traditionally believed in an economy where those who make a contribution are rewarded. A man like Jaiyeola should be able to work eight hours at Sears and then go home.

LOW PRICES, LOW PAYCHECK

Cons argue that we have to choose between having high wages and having low prices. They are wrong.

Take the case of Wal-Mart. According to the United Food and Commercial Workers union (UFCW), Wal-Mart could pay each employee a dollar more per hour if the company increased its prices by a half penny per dollar. For example, a $2 pair of socks would then cost $2.01. This minimal increase would add up to $1,800 annually for each employee.

I wouldn't mind paying more for a pair of socks if it meant that my fellow Americans would be able to pay for good health care. That would save me money because right now Wal-Mart's uninsured employees run up hundreds of thousands of dollars in bills at emergency treatment centers when their problems often could have been solved more cheaply and with better results had they been caught earlier at a doctor's office.

And I wouldn't mind paying one cent more for a pair of socks if it meant that parents could be home at night and on the weekends spending quality time with their kids. That's a real family value.

Here's what all this talk about wages really comes down to: Would you rather pay 10 percent more at Wal-Mart and get 30 percent more in your paycheck, or would you rather have lower prices and an even lower paycheck? That's the real choice: we're either spiraling up into a strong middle class, or we're spiraling down toward serfdom.

Looking at the arc of U.S. history, we discover we've been on a downward spiral ever since Ronald Reagan declared war on working people in 1981. Companies cut prices and then cut wages so they can still turn a hefty profit. Folks whose wages have been cut can't afford to shop at midrange stores like Macy's, so they have to buy at "low-wage" discount stores like Wal-Mart. That drives more midrange stores out of business and increases pressure on discount stores to send their prices even lower. To compensate for lower prices, they lower wages so they can still turn a hefty profit. On and on it goes—until the people working those jobs are no longer middle class and have to work two or three jobs to survive.

Our choice is not between low prices at Wal-Mart and high prices at Wal-Mart. It's between low prices at Wal-Mart with lousy paychecks and no protection for labor, and the prices Wal-Mart had when Sam Walton ran the company and nearly everything was made in the United States and people had good union jobs and decent paychecks.

The choice is ultimately about whether we want to have a middle class in this country.

THE REAL JOBS/SALARY EQUATION

Rush Limbaugh tells his listeners that if we raise the minimum wage, small businesses will go under and the country will lose jobs. History tells us that that is nonsense. The reality is that every time the minimum wage gets raised, employment goes up.

For example, when Santa Fe, New Mexico, voted to raise the minimum wage to $9.50, the cons screamed that the economy would go south. It didn't. According to living-wage advocates Monsignor Jerome Martinez and City Councilor David Coss, the number of recipients of Temporary Aid to Needy Families has fallen 9.7 percent since the wage increase, while in the state as a whole it had gone down only 0.6 percent. Further, they write in ABQjournal.com:

We have gained jobs. According to a Sept. 22 report from the New Mexico Department of Labor, 1,400 jobs have been added to the Santa Fe work force since the living wage came into effect. This 2.3 percent rate of job growth is a little more than the state's 2.1 percent job growth rate during this same period. Santa Fe's 2.3 percent growth rate is very high, as the state's job growth, at 2.1 percent, ranked 12th highest in the country.

The hospitality industry in Santa Fe did even better, adding 300 jobs, a 3.2 percent growth rate. The unemployment rate in Santa Fe in August was 3.8 percent, down from 4.1 percent a year ago. The Santa Fe rate is much better than the state as a whole, which had 5.3 percent unemployment last month.[4]

America has the money. It's just a question of how we use it. A caller to my radio program once offered a good example. He was arguing against raising wages. He posed a problem of an investor who would like to develop property. He asked me, "Would it be better to pay ten carpenters $20 per hour and build one building, or pay twenty carpenters $10 per hour and build two buildings?" Wouldn't it be better for the economy, he said, to employ more people?

The question my caller missed was this: Do you want to have a middle class in the community in which you are building? That is, do you want there to be people who can afford to live in your building and shop at the stores you may develop? If the answer is yes, you better pay a living wage and build one building.

431 TIMES THE REST OF US

Let's turn this question around the other way. Let's ask the cons: Would it be better to pay ten executives $100,000 per year and invest the rest of the company's profits in the company and its workers and shareholders; or would it be better to pay ten executives $1 million per year and claim you'd gotten the best leadership money could buy?

The nation's top executives now make an average of $11.8 million per year—each. That's just their salary; it doesn't count bonuses, perks, stock options, and so forth. For example, the *Washington Post* tells us in a June 27, 2005, story that many top executives get whatever they ask for. The article cites several examples, among them the case of a health-care executive:

> Coventry Health Care Inc., an HMO company, gave chairman and former chief executive Allen F. Wise a deal that includes as much as $12,000 for legal, tax and financial planning, an unspecified automobile allowance, 75 hours of personal airplane use and a "tax equalization bonus" to ensure that those other benefits entail "no net cost to him," according to a regulatory filing.

Why do executives making $11 million per year need an automobile allowance? Can't they pay for their own financial planning?

Even some executives are starting to feel uncomfortable about all this excess. The *Post* interviewed William W. George, former chief executive of Medtronic Inc. and a member of the boards of such companies as Goldman Sachs and Exxon Mobil, who expressed concern about high executive salaries: "Executives make a lot of money," he told the *Post*, "so they ought to be able to pay for those things themselves. . . . How far do you want to go? Groceries?"

Executives' pay is now 431 times what their employees make on average ($27,460). United for a Fair Economy writes in its *Executive Excess 2005* report: "If the minimum wage had risen as fast as CEO pay since 1990, the lowest paid workers in the U.S. would be earning $23.03 an hour today, not $5.15 an hour."[5]

Our economy has plenty of money, but the money is going to the corporatocracy, to the richest among us, instead of to the millions of people who—as Abraham Lincoln pointed out—actually make the country work. A living wage would be a first step toward equalizing this balance and resecuring an American middle class.

But a living wage is just a starting point. Even people making a "living wage" often must work two jobs. To support a middle class in this country, we need universal single-payer health-care coverage. We need to strengthen Social Security, not weaken it. We need to offer a free, high-quality public education.

And one of the best ways we get all that for American workers is by supporting unions.

WHY UNIONS?

Unless you are a CEO, you don't have a lot of leverage to demand benefits at your workplace. Every year or two, you might go to your boss and ask for a raise or an extra day of vacation, but usually you can't do much about what hours you work, what health benefits you receive, or how your retirement benefits are structured. Unions give workers that leverage.

Unions are designed to give workers a voice in decisions that affect their jobs. They allow workers to negotiate with their employers for wages, health benefits, retirement benefits, and good working conditions. In the best circumstances, unions partner with companies—both have an interest in satisfied, happy workers.

Unions create a middle class by allowing you and me to ask for the wages and the benefits we need to become or remain middle class. Unionized workers earn higher wages, have better benefits, enjoy greater job stability, and work in a safer environment. In 2003 union workers earned an average of 27 percent more than nonunionized workers. Seventy-three percent of union workers received medical benefits compared with just 51 percent of nonunion workers. And 79 percent of union workers have pension plans.

Cons have slandered unions for more than a hundred years. Professional people have bought the line that it is unprofessional to be in a union, that only blue-collar workers unionize. People worried about their status and legitimacy—like nurses—tend not to join unions.

But it's not true that unions are just for blue-collar workers. Unions are for anyone who wants to be middle class. Teachers are almost all unionized. Actors—most of whom are not Sean Penn or Charlize Theron and don't get paid big bucks—are almost all unionized. Anyone who works needs the rights that unions can provide.

DEMOCRACY IN THE WORKPLACE

Most of us don't think about workplace rights. We assume that because we live in America, we have all the rights we need.

There are no constitutional protections in the workplace. Most people are at-will employees, which means they can be hired or fired at will. Federal law protects you from being fired because of race, age, gender, or disability, but it doesn't protect you from being fired for saying that the boss is overworking you or the company's actions are immoral. You can't say that sort of thing in the workplace because the workplace is not a democracy.

Why does that matter?

If you can't talk freely about your working conditions, you can't negotiate changes to those conditions. If you're afraid the boss will fire you if you complain about overtime, you have no way to prevent your boss from requiring you to work extra hours.

We have a democracy in this country because the Founders realized that they could not change the king of England's lousy taxation system unless they had representation in government. Democracy gives us the power to create a society that matches our needs. Democracy in the workplace allows us to negotiate the conditions of our work. It ensures that honest working people like Muyiwa Jaiyeola can be middle class without having to work sixty hours per week.

According to Thea M. Lee, assistant director of public policy for the American Federation of Labor and the Congress of Industrial Organizations (AFL-CIO), for there to be democracy in the workplace, workers must have fundamental rights. These rights include freedom of association—which means the right to organize and bargain collectively—and prohibitions on child labor, forced labor, and discrimination in employment.

You may think that we have all of these rights now. We don't. U.S. workers have almost no right to organize. Every twenty-three minutes in the United States, a worker is either fired or harassed for trying to unionize. Our president goes around the world, talking about the importance of bringing democracy. We loved Lech Walesa and his union movement in Poland. But today, if the middle class is to survive, we need a Lech Walesa in the United States—or at least some honest education about our own country's labor history.

LABOR IN AMERICA

Labor goes back a long way in U.S. history. In 1874 unemployed workers were demonstrating in New York City's Tompkins Square Park. Riot police moved in and began beating men, women, and children with billy clubs, leaving hundreds of casualties in their wake. The police commissioner said: "It was the most glorious sight I ever saw."

Three years later, on June 18, 1877, ten coal-mining activists were hanged. That same year a general strike in Chicago—called the Battle of the Viaduct—halted the movement of U.S. railroads across the states. Federal troops were called up, and they killed thirty workers and wounded more than a hundred.

In September 1882 thirty thousand workers marched in the first-ever Labor Day in New York history. In 1884 the Federation of Organized Trades and Labor Unions was established, and it passed a resolution stating that eight hours should constitute a legal day's work. Hundreds of thousands of American workers began following that rule.

In May 1, 1886, the Knights of Labor took to the streets to call for an eight-hour day. Eighty thousand workers shut down the city of Chicago. On May 4 three thousand workers gathered in Haymarket Square. A bomb was thrown that killed seven policemen. Eight of the people present were rounded up, tried for murder, and sentenced to death. The Haymarket riot became the symbol of labor injustice in America.

This is but a fragment of the history of the labor movement in the United States.

Matters improved when labor got organized—but not much. In fact, by the 1920s things looked a lot like they do today: the robber barons were in charge, and the situation for working people was bleak. The rich were incredibly rich, and the few middle-class workers were deeply in debt. The labor movement appeared virtually dead.

It took the Republican Great Depression to wake people up. It took Franklin D. Roosevelt to speak the truth. If a politician said the same things today that Roosevelt did in the 1930s—openly accusing big business of being anti-American and antiworker—he'd be accused of socialism and communism. Very few national figures have the courage to speak out today the way FDR did back then.

Roosevelt provided courageous leadership. In his first term, he had sent to Congress the National Industrial Recovery Act, which set standards for wages and working hours and established the right of laborers to organize. This set the stage for labor groups to bargain for wages and conditions. Thanks in large part to FDR's work on behalf of labor, in the twenty-five years after World War II the real incomes of the middle class doubled.

WHY WE NEED A LABOR MOVEMENT TODAY

Today America is regressing. Middle-class income has stopped growing. The net worth of those who earn less than $150,000 per year (which includes everybody from the working poor to the highest end of the most well-off of the middle class) is down by 0.6 percent.

The problem isn't the economy. Corporations are making more money than ever. The real income of people whose net worth exceeds $100 million is *doubling.*

What's happening is simple: the rich are getting richer and the entire spectrum of the middle class is disappearing.

We can easily trace this decline to Reagan's first public declaration of war on the middle class when he went after the Professional Air Traffic Controllers Organization (PATCO) in 1981. He broke the back of the air-traffic controllers' union and began the practice of using the Department of Labor—traditionally the ally of workers—against organized labor and working people.

Reagan liked to say he was against "big government." What he really meant was that he was against Roosevelt's New Deal. He was against Social Security, the minimum wage, free college education (he ended that in California as its governor), and programs like the WPA. He believed in the discredited concept of "trickledown" economics—the theory that if you create a corporatocracy, the rich will nobly spend some of their money to help the rest of us.

The American people don't need handouts. Our workers just want to be paid a living wage for a fair day's work. We can't count on the corporatocracy to give us what we earn, so we need a strong labor movement to give us the power to negotiate our wages and benefits.

Ultimately, it's all about power.

Workplaces are not democracies—in the United States they're run more like kingdoms. Employers have the power to hire and fire, to raise or lower wages, to change working conditions and job responsibilities, and to change hours and times and places. Workers have only the power to work or to not work (known as a strike).

The strike—a tool that can effectively be used only by *organized* labor—is the only means by which workers can address the extreme imbalance of power in the workplace. And because organized labor *is* a democracy—leadership is elected and strike decisions and contracts are voted on—unions bring more democracy to America. We spend about half our waking lives at work—at least we can have some democracy in the workplace; and a democracy means a strong middle class.

THE ENERGY SOLUTION

Another way the middle class is getting screwed is by energy prices. While wages and salaries have been in a slow, gradual decline since trickle-down economics was reinflicted on this nation in 2001, the cost of getting to and from work has exploded.   ·

In part this is because we're now at or approaching a time of "peak oil," which I discuss at length in my book *The Last Hours of Ancient Sunlight.* During the Carboniferous Period 300 to 400 million years ago, plants captured about 100 million years' worth of sunlight. They stored this sunlight energy through the chemical process of photosynthesis, locking it into molecules containing carbon from the atmosphere and hydrogen and oxygen from water, which became the bodies of the plants. These carbohydrates—plant matter, from both land plants and huge mats of sea plants—were forced deep into the earth, where under great pressure and over time they converted into coal, oil, and natural gas.

The problem we face is threefold.

First, there is a finite amount of stored "ancient sunlight" in the ground, particularly in the form of natural gas and oil. With regard to oil, most in the industry subscribe to oil scientist L. King Hubbard's hypothesis that once about half of the oil in a well is drained out, the well has "peaked" and the remaining half is going to get harder—and more expensive—to extract. The United States hit a "Hubbard's peak" in the 1970s, and most scientists agree that the world is hitting one about now, and this is reflected in volatility in the world's oil markets.

Second, releasing the energy of ancient sunlight into the world not only reliberates 400-million-year-old sun energy as heat but also reliberates the carbon that was scrubbed from the atmosphere back then to store that heat/energy. This carbon, released from burning oil, coal, and natural gas, mostly takes the form of carbon dioxide, a "greenhouse gas" that contributes to global warming.

Third, and perhaps most significant to today's middle-class working people, is that for three decades we have had the technology to largely abandon fossil fuels, but our politicians have failed us.

In 1979 President Jimmy Carter declared an energy emergency and established programs to quickly wean the United States off its dependence on imported oil. He set up a series of research supports, market interventions, and tax breaks for homeowners who "went solar" so that by the year 2000 the United States would derive 20 percent of its total energy from solar power. Had his programs remained in effect, we would not have the crisis we have today, and the birthing of a new alternative-energy industry with a little stimulus from government could have driven an economic boom that would make the dot-com days look modest.

Unfortunately, Ronald Reagan and oilman George H. W. Bush were brought into office on the wings of big-oil money. They removed Carter's solar collectors from the roof of the White House, cut and later eliminated the alternative-energy tax credits and research programs, and even opposed modest programs like increasing average manufactured-car fuel-efficiency standards. The needle was inserted into our national vein, and to this day we remain, in the words of Bush Jr., "addicted to oil."

The good news is that it's still possible to recapture Jimmy Carter's vision of an energy-self-sufficient America. And if we undertake this with vigor and enthusiasm, it'll become a new goal and standard for the world as well. Rebuild our mass transit systems, revive our railroads, decentralize our power plants, and shift to solar, wind, geothermal, biomass, and wave power. Develop world-class technologies to make hybrid and renewable-fuel vehicles and give the two remaining domestic automakers strong incentives to bring them to market inexpensively. Mandate energy-saving features in new appliances and the manufacture of new homes.

None of this is rocket science—it's all within the means of current technology. It simply requires that we have politicians in Washington who are willing to stand up to the lobbyists from big oil and advocate for America's middle class and, ultimately, all of humanity.

To-do List

The cons have almost succeeded in throttling American democracy by screwing over the middle class. To fight back we must battle on two fronts.

First, we must recognize and reclaim the government programs that create a middle class:

▶ Return to the American people our ownership of the military, the prison system, and the ballot box.

▶ Fight for free and public education that encourages critical thinking, historical knowledge, and a love of learning in each child. Combat the No Child Left Behind Act and the belief that education is a commodity that can be tested.

▶ Fight for a national single-payer health-care system based on Medicare.

▶ Fight for Social Security—do not let it be privatized or co-opted.

▶ Fight for progressive taxation: reinstate a rate of 35 percent on corporations and a rate of 70 percent on the wealthiest 5 percent of Americans—and use the money to pay back the Social Security system and to fund an economic investment program.

▶ Fight for a living wage and for the right of labor to organize.

▶ Fight for a national energy program that puts people and the planet—not Big Oil—first.

When America has a strong middle class, democracy will follow. The opposite is also true.

To fight back we must also make use of the ballot box. We can achieve the economic programs that make the middle class possible by using the power of our democracy to vote for those politicians who support the middle class.

We've been conned for long enough. It's time to take back America.

The Road to Victory

Back in 2003, when my "progressive talk radio" program was first nationally syndicated on Sirius Satellite Radio and about two dozen stations around the country, one of our regular listeners was a guy I knew only as "Jeff in Denver." During the first year of the show, Jeff's constant call and complaint was that the Democratic Party in his area "was lost, had no vision, was too corporate and conservative, and was just letting itself get run over."

One day I challenged him, saying something to the effect of, "If you don't like what they're doing, why don't you show up at one of their meetings and let them know?"

Months went by, and one day Jeff called again. He'd shown up at his local county Democratic Party caucus. There were about a dozen people there, most of them in their midforties or older and showing—in Jeff's opinion—a "lack of knowledge of issues, lack of vision, and lack of time put in deciding issues."

Jeff got active in the party and, to make a long story short, was responsible (along with a few compatriots) for moving his party in a more progressive direction at both the local and state levels. He's now "working to develop an issue-by-issue platform for the party, creating tools for activists, writing a definitive vocabulary (to counter [Frank] Luntz), and creating a do-it-yourself guide for rEvolution (peaceful yet dramatic change)." All because he showed up and got involved.

Lupita and the Oregon Democrats

In 2005 I was the keynote speaker at the annual meeting of the Washington County, Oregon, Democratic Party. Lupita Maurer, the party chair, told me how just four years earlier the Washington County Democrats had been lucky to draw two dozen people to a meeting. There were more than three hundred at the meeting I addressed, and it wasn't because I was the speaker—that's how much the party had grown since it had been infiltrated by activists.

A longtime member of the Washington County Democratic Party told me, "For a lot of years, it was just fifteen or so of the old stalwarts, people who stuck with the party through thick and thin, no matter how bad things looked; they could be relied on, and they were there and kept it alive. But then both Howard Dean and Dennis Kucinich launched campaigns that energized people, bringing them into the party. And even after the campaigns, they've continued to participate and have revitalized the local Democratic Party."

In early 2006 they opened their first-ever local headquarters office, where people can drop in, organize, participate, and get information about what the party's doing—or tell the Party what they think it should do.

Roy in Rio Rancho

In early 2006 "Roy in Rio Rancho, New Mexico" called my program. He had recently gotten involved in local politics, he said, in part because of the excesses of the Bush administration and in part because he "was inspired by that guy from Colorado who called your show a few years ago and got active."

Roy was brimming with enthusiasm: "New Mexico now has verifiable paper ballots for every election in the state." He said:

> Some serious guys did some serious work: they created the parade, and the governor got out in front of it. Fortunately, we had a Democratic governor and a Democratically controlled Round House because it was pretty much a party-line vote, but it went down about six hours before the session closed. It's not perfect, but at least we've now got ballots that we can look at and we can recount.

It turned out Roy was one of those "serious guys." He'd shown up for a Democratic Party meeting in his community. "Now I'm a Democratic precinct vice-chair; I'm the vice president of the county Democratic Club."

Roy wrapped up his call with a message to our listeners: "The main reason I called in is to say that when you just get down and you feel like you've been kicked in the teeth, just keep on pitching. Get out there and just agitate! Get the word out around the country, Thom! People, just get out there! Heck, it's fun!"

Roy is right. Jeff and Roy are Democrats, but Roy's message is a call to all patriotic Americans, regardless of party affiliation. Democrat, Republican, or Green—if you are being screwed by the cons, it's time to get involved. It's time that We the People took back control of our government.

TAKING BACK THE DEMOCRATIC PARTY

Over the past decade, progressives have spent a lot of time on the outside, looking in. There are undeniable benefits to being an outsider: it's much easier to criticize what you don't like than to change it.

It's vital to point out slanted reporting in the corporate media, but it's also important to seize enough political power in Washington to enforce antitrust laws to break up media monopolies.

It's critical to detail the failures of the cons' policies, but we should also take on the oil wars, endemic corporate cronyism, slashed environmental regulations, and corporate-controlled voting machines. We need to work toward replacing an administration that daily gives the big pharma, HMO, banking, and insurance industries whatever they want regardless of how many people are harmed.

This lack of political power is a crisis others have faced before. We should learn from their experience.

After the crushing defeat of Barry Goldwater in 1964, a similar crisis faced a loose coalition of gun lovers, abortion foes, southern segregationists, Ayn Rand libertarians, proto-Moonies, and those who feared that immigration within and communism without would destroy the America they loved. Each of these various groups had tried its own direct-action tactics, from demonstrations and pamphleteering to organizing and fielding candidates. None succeeded in gaining mainstream recognition or affecting American political processes. If anything, their efforts led to their being branded "special interest" or "fringe" groups, which further diminished their political power.

Instead of getting angry, these cons decided to get power.

They decided that the only way to seize control of the American political agenda was to infiltrate and take over one of the two national political parties, using their own think tanks like the Coors-funded Heritage Foundation to mold public opinion along the way. Now they regularly get their spokespeople on radio and television talk shows and newscasts, and they write a steady stream of daily op-ed pieces for national newspapers.

They launched an aggressive takeover of Dwight Eisenhower's "moderate" Republican Party, opening up the "big tent" to invite in groups that had previously been considered on the fringe. Archconservative neo-Christians who argue that the Bible should replace the Constitution even funded the startup of a corporation to manufacture computer-controlled voting machines, which are now installed across the nation.[1] And former weapons manufacturer and current ultraconservative cult leader Reverend Sun Myung Moon took over the *Washington Times* newspaper and UPI.

Their efforts, as we see today, have borne fruit, as Kevin P. Phillips predicted they would in his prescient 1969 book *The Emerging Republican Majority* and as David Brock so well documents in his book *Blinded by the Right: The Conscience of an Ex-conservative.*

In response to the cons' takeover of the Republican Party and of American politics, the Democratic Party also swung to the right. Ask any Green or Progressive or left-leaning Reform Party member and they will tell you: "The Democrats have just become weaker versions of the Republicans!"

True enough, in many cases. And leaning to the right isn't working for the Democrats because, as Democrat Harry Truman said, "When voters are given a choice between voting for a Republican, or a Democrat who acts like a Republican, they'll vote for the Republican every time." (And history shows that voters are equally uninterested in Republicans who act like Democrats.)

How have progressives responded to the Democrats' swing to the right? Instead of taking a page from the cons and funding think tanks to influence public opinion, subsidizing radio and TV talk-show hosts nationwide, and working to take over the Democratic Party, many defected to create their own parties while others gave up on mainstream politics altogether.

The remaining Democrats were caught in the awkward position of needing to embrace the same corporate donors as the con-led Republicans, although they weren't anywhere near as successful as the cons because they hadn't (and haven't) so fully sold out to corporate and wealthy interests.

As a result, the Democratic Party is facing a crisis right now. A few Democratic stalwarts survive who may oppose Bush and the cons on the national stage; but while the rest of us fixate on the cons' war in Iraq, the cons are creeping into the very heart of Jefferson's party, using lobbyist money and campaign slush funds as their way in.

Thus the best immediate solution to advance the progressive agenda is for progressives to join and take back the Democratic Party in the same way cons seized control of the Republican Party.

WHAT ABOUT CREATING A THIRD PARTY?

Alternative parties have an important place in American politics, and those in them should continue to work for their strength and vitality. They're essential as incubators of ideas and nexus points for activism. That does not mean, however, that they are an alternative to the two mainstream parties when election time rolls around.

Those on the right learned this lesson well. Many groups that in the past had fielded their own candidates stopped fielding candidates but remain intact and have become powerful influences on the Republican Party. Similarly, being a Green doesn't mean you can't also be a Democrat.

The fact that America is fundamentally a two-party country is not a popular truth. There's a long list of people who didn't want to believe it—Teddy Roosevelt, H. Ross Perot, John Anderson, Pat Buchanan, and Ralph Nader, to name but a few.

The United States—the first functioning democracy in the modern world—seems able to support only two parties, while democratic countries like Germany, India, and Israel have three, four, or even more. The reason is that in America—unlike most other modern democracies—we have regional "winner take all" elections rather than proportional representation. It's written right into our Constitution. The Founders rarely made mistakes, but "winner take all" elections were a whopper.

Here's what it means: say a country is leaning left, with 60 percent of the voters preferring left-wing candidates and

40 percent of the voters preferring right-wing candidates. In a system with proportional representation, people vote by party, and legislatures are created based on the proportion each party receives. So if 30 percent of the people vote for the Green Party and 30 percent vote for the Democrats and 40 percent vote for the Republicans, 30 percent of the legislators will be Greens, 30 percent will be Democrats, and 40 percent will be Republicans. The Greens and the Democrats can then band together if they want to put forth a left-wing agenda.

In a "winner take all" system, however, people vote for individual representatives, and whoever has the most votes gets all of the pie. Say 60 percent of the people in a state want a left-wing senator. If two left-wing candidates, one a Democrat and one a Green, split the left-wing vote (30 percent and 30 percent), however, the Republican candidate wins with 40 percent of the vote. The left-wing voters lose. If that happens enough times in enough elections, the legislature can end up having a Republican majority even if most of the people are Greens and Democrats.

We see the result of the "winner take all" system in races across the nation, such as my former home state of Vermont. In the 2002 election for governor and lieutenant governor, the people who voted for the Democratic and Progressive candidates constituted a clear majority. Nonetheless, the Republican candidates for governor and lieutenant governor were elected with 45 percent and 41 percent of the vote, respectively, because each had more votes than his Democratic or Progressive opponents alone. (Example: Republican Brian Dubie—41 percent; Democrat Peter Shumlin—32 percent; Progressive Anthony Pollina—25 percent. The Republican won.)

Similarly, Republicans have overtly used third-party participation on the left to their advantage. In a July 2002 story in the *Washington Post,* writer Thomas B. Edsall noted: "The chairman of the Republican Party of New Mexico said yesterday he was approached by a GOP figure who asked him to offer the state Green

Party at least $100,000 to run candidates in two contested congres-sional districts in an effort to divide the Democratic vote."[2]

The Republicans well understand and exploit the fact that in the U.S. electoral system a third-party candidate will always be a detriment to the major-party candidate with whom he or she is most closely aligned.

The Australians solved this problem in the past decade by instituting nationwide instant run-off voting (IRV), a system that is making inroads in communities across the United States. There are also efforts to reform our electoral system along the lines of other democratic nations, instituting proportional representation systems such as first proposed by John Stuart Mill in 1861 and now adopted by virtually every democracy in the world except the United States, Australia, Greece, the United Kingdom, and Canada.

These are good and important efforts for the long-term fu-ture of American democracy, but they don't solve the immediate problem. If you don't think your local party is doing a good job, by all means go ahead and form an alternative. But don't stop there. Also join your local Democratic or Republican party. Put your energy into taking your mainstream party back so that on election day your representative really represents you!

REPUBLICANS: TAKE BACK YOUR PARTY, TOO!

Today's so-called Republicans have established a mind-numbing record of polluting the environment; bloating government; ap-pointing crony partisans; pushing the nation into debt to fund tax cuts for the rich; legislatively catering to the world's largest corporations; opposing women's rights; kneecapping states, local communities, and schools; eviscerating constitutional protections of liberty at home; and devastating our nation's reputation abroad.

Corporate shills like former Enron lobbyist and GOP chair Ed Gillespie would have us think that the Republican Party was born in service to corporations. But Abraham Lincoln, the first

Republican president, was also the first president to actively use the power of government in support of striking workers.

In Lincoln's era the idea of strikes was so novel that the word *strike* was put in quotation marks in newspapers, but Lincoln was often on the side of the strikers. "Labor," Lincoln wrote, "is prior to, and independent of, capital. Capital is only the fruit of labor, and could never have existed if labor had not first existed. Labor is superior to capital, and deserves much the higher consideration."

Republicans would do well to revisit the Republican Party's campaign platform of 1872—before the Republican railroad bribery scandals of the late 1870s and 1880s corrupted the party—as it may hold the seeds of their redemption.

The Republicans of 1872 didn't think that anybody should be appointed to high office just because he was a party hack or the son of the secretary of state. Instead, they wrote in their national party platform, "Any system of civil service under which the subordinate positions of the government are considered rewards for mere party zeal is fatally demoralizing; and we, therefore, favor a reform of the system, by laws which shall abolish the evils of patronage, and make honesty, efficiency, and fidelity the essential qualifications for public positions."

They didn't think corporations—particularly big ones—should get the kinds of freebies that corporations today regularly demand for moving into a community. Instead, resources owned by We the People should be held in trust for, or given to, human beings, as they wrote in their platform: "We are opposed to further grants of public land to corporations and monopolies, and demand that the national domain be set apart for free homes for the people."

The Republicans of 1872 felt that the national debt (from the Civil War) should be paid off as quickly as possible, and a budget must not only be balanced but show a surplus while at the same time paying pensions to retired persons. They were also protectionists, in favor of import duties and tariffs to protect working people's salaries and keep manufacturing jobs from moving off-shore. They proclaimed in their platform:

> The [nation's] annual revenue, after paying current expenditures, pensions, and the interest on the public debt, should furnish a moderate balance for the reduction of the principal [of the national debt]; and that revenue should be raised by duties upon importations, the details of which [duties] should be so adjusted as to aid in securing remunerative wages to labor, and promote the industries, prosperity, and growth of the whole country.

The Republicans of 1872 had repealed most of Lincoln's wartime arrogations of civil rights and opposed any other Patriot Act–like interferences with civil liberties. They were rediscovering the Bill of Rights—and said so in party platform plank sixteen:

> The Republican party proposes to respect the rights reserved by the people to themselves as carefully as the powers delegated by them to the States and the Federal government. It disapproves of the resort to unconstitutional laws for the purpose of removing evils, by interference with rights not surrendered by the people to either the State or National government.

The party platform said that Republicans would embrace only "modest patriotism" and "incorruptible integrity" in their leaders because the nation's "honor" was, in that day, "kept in the high respect throughout the world."

They added, perhaps presciently, "We believe the people will not entrust the government to any party or combination of men composed chiefly of those who have resisted every step of such beneficent progress."

In the years since then, the Republican Party has been seized by Ayn Rand utopians, Pat Robertson fundamentalists, and the largest and dirtiest of America's corporate elite. They've trashed the values of Lincoln and Eisenhower, rejected Jesus' words in Matthew 25,[3] and turned our commons into a dumping ground while using our nation's Treasury as an ATM for themselves and their cronies.

Even conservative Republicans like former *Wall Street Journal* editor and Reagan administration assistant Treasury secretary Paul C. Roberts are concerned that the current crop of so-called Republicans are on the verge of destroying the last vestiges of American civil society, wiping out our middle class, and permanently turning our nation into the land of the observed and the home of the worried-about-the-terror-alert.

So, those of us "on the left" must ask of our Republican friends: please take your party back from these fanatics before it's too late for America to ever again be the land of the free and the home of the brave.

CHANGE HAPPENS—BUT SOMETIMES SLOWLY

My old friend Paul Rogat Loeb has written many books of great value, and one of my favorites is his *Soul of a Citizen,* in which he reminds us of the importance of doing the sometimes dull, boring, difficult daily work if we really are to save this great nation.

"A few years ago, on Martin Luther King Day," Paul writes,

> I was interviewed on CNN along with Rosa Parks. "Rosa Parks was the woman who wouldn't go to the back of the bus," said the host. "That set in motion the yearlong bus boycott in Montgomery. It earned Rosa Parks the title of 'mother of the civil rights movement.'"

> The host's description—the standard rendition of the story—stripped the boycott of its context. Before refusing to give up her bus seat to a white person, Parks had spent 12 years helping to lead the local NAACP chapter. The summer before, she had attended a 10-day training session at the Highlander Center, Tennessee's labor and civil rights organizing school, where she'd met older activists and discussed the Supreme Court decision banning "separate but equal" schools.

Parks had become familiar with previous challenges to segregation: another Montgomery bus boycott, 50 years earlier; a bus boycott in Baton Rouge two years before Parks was arrested; and an NAACP dilemma the previous spring, when a young Montgomery woman had also refused to move to the back of the bus. The NAACP had considered a legal challenge but decided the unmarried, pregnant woman would be a poor symbol for a campaign.

In short, Parks didn't make a spur-of-the-moment decision. She was part of a movement for change at a time when success was far from certain. This in no way diminishes her historical importance, but it reminds us that this powerful act might never have taken place without the humble, frustrating work that preceded it.[4]

In his books and speeches, Loeb reminds us over and over again that activism isn't just showing up for a peace rally and marching down the street once, or making an annual phone call to your member of Congress. It's about participating—in a deep, visceral, and meaningful way—in the ongoing process of awakening America and transforming our political landscape.

OTHER ACTIVIST TOOLS

The most fundamental tool of activism is communication. The American Revolution wouldn't have been possible were it not for two simple forms of communication: letters to the editors and pamphlets (what we would call "op-ed pieces"). As a result of such communications, in just a few short years—largely from the Boston Tea Party in 1773 to the Declaration of Independence in 1776—American public opinion swung from being opposed to a revolutionary war to being sufficiently in favor of it that the general populace would hide and support soldiers fighting a largely insurgent war against the British army.

Letters to the editor are still powerful devices to influence public opinion; and a little-known but significant dimension of them is that while they're not read by a majority of newspaper readers, they *are* read by most politicians. A letter to the editor of your local newspaper about a particular issue—especially if it mentions a politician by name—will have far more impact on that politician and his or her views than calls, faxes, letters, or e-mails to the politician's office.

The Internet offers other ways to get involved. Message boards, online forums, blog responses, and the like have become so effective that several of the cons' think tanks actually pay people to participate in online discussion areas to promote their ideas or candidates. (My own online message board has had postings from several of these hired guns over the past three years—with a flurry of them just before the 2004 election.)

While I don't know of any progressive foundations or think tanks that are paying people to post ideas and messages in favor of progressive candidates on the cons' boards, it's certainly important work. If you have the time and can stand the association with the often-bigoted crowds that populate the message boards of the cons' Web sites and talk-show hosts, your voice may help awaken a few people.

The second tool used by the colonists of 1773 to awaken and galvanize the nation was pamphlets. Usually single sheets of paper with a large headline and a short message, they pointed out the ills of British occupation and called for action. The quotes earlier in this book from "Rusticus"—one of America's early pamphleteers—are classic examples of this technique. The pamphlets would be nailed to public buildings and trees in public places overnight, slipped under people's doors, and passed from person to person.

The modern equivalent of Revolutionary-era pamphleteering in print is writing op-eds and producing "zines," but it mainly occurs now on the Internet—creating individual Web sites, starting your own blog, forwarding e-mails, and the like. Another variation is to call talk-radio shows—particularly ones run by cons—and put forward your views. Using the electronic media that was unavailable to the Founders is a powerful way to speed up the process of awakening America to the war on the middle class and what we can do about it.

CALL YOUR CONGRESSIONAL REPRESENTATIVES

Contacting your elected representatives is vital work. The Founders of this nation and the Framers of the Constitution were very clear that we don't elect *leaders* in America—we elect *representatives*. For example, from time to time I've had as guests on my radio program politicians who've taken positions on issues with which I disagree. The bottom line for me, though, is that if they are truly representing the desires and the interests of their state or district, I can't condemn them for taking those positions. That, after all, is what they're elected to do. (On the other hand, many make that claim when it's patently false, such as those who supported the so-called bankruptcy reform legislation in 2005, which benefited only people wealthy enough to have an Asset Protection Trust to shelter their money from bankruptcy or the banking industry.)

Given that our senators and members of the House of Representatives (and more-local politicians, all the way down to school board members) are elected to *represent* our will rather than *lead* us, it's important that we let them know how we feel, what our vision is, and what story we want them acting out. The best way to do this is to show up at public events where they're present and speak out. And if your elected officials aren't showing up much in public, create a venue for them.

Rep. Bernie Sanders (Independent, VT)—who's been a weekly guest on my program for more than two years—has often suggested to listeners that if there is an issue about which they're passionate, they should get together at least fifty or a hundred people who'll commit to showing up, book a hall or a school au-ditorium, and invite their senator or congressperson to come for a Town Hall meeting. Politicians who consistently refuse to meet with their own constituents should be voted out of office.

Politicians I know tell me that the communications from their constituents that are most compelling are those that are handwritten or clearly unique typewritten letters. When writing to a politician, keep it short, clear, and to the point. Open with your specific concern and close with a call to action. Don't make it more than a single page. A single paragraph is even better.

If writing about multiple issues, write multiple letters as some politicians—particularly at the national level—file letters according to topic. (One senatorial staffer told me that they stack and weigh letters on an issue, pro and con; whichever stack weighs more tells that senator how his constituents feel. If true, maybe we should be writing our letters on coated paper stock as it's much heavier than normal paper!)

Next on the list are faxes and phone calls. You can easily google the phone number of your elected representatives; and the main switchboard on Capitol Hill—which will connect you to the office of any member of the House, the Senate, or the White House—is (202) 225-3121. Several organizations also pay for toll-free numbers that connect to this number. As with letters, keep faxes and phone calls short, polite, and to the point. Odds are the result of your call will simply be a single check mark on a list that reads something like "ANWAR Drilling—For or Against," so don't try to convert or enlighten the staffer or intern who's answering the phone. (That's best done with your letter to the editor.)

Members of the U.S. House of Representatives and the U.S. Senate will always give higher priority to people from their own district, so when calling your own representative or senators, be sure to give your name and ZIP code (and address, if you want to get their mailings).

Some members are on powerful committees that influence the entire nation, so if you're calling a member who doesn't directly represent you, you may want to mention that his or her activities on that particular committee do, in fact, affect all Americans, so on this particular issue you feel that the politician *does* represent you and should hear your voice, too.

JOIN THE UNION MOVEMENT

Even if your workplace isn't unionized, it's still possible to involve yourself with the union movement. The two largest umbrella organizations in the union movement are the AFL-CIO and Change to Win. You can get on Change to Win's e-mailing list by entering your information on its Web site at www.changetowin.org.

The AFL-CIO has gone a step further and created a union-affiliated organization for people who aren't represented by a union but want to support the union movement and participate in its work and goals. It's called Working America, and you can join at www.workingamerica.com.

One of the most important keys to rebuilding America's middle class, though, is to strengthen and re-empower its union movement through legislative changes. Our laws define the rules of the game of business, and they define the relationship between employer and employee. They make possible unionization *and* union busting. In the absence of laws protecting workers' rights, the power of capital will always crush the power of workers.

Thus, it's vital to elect union-friendly politicians to public office.

In 1947, after Republicans took the House and the Senate in the election of 1946, they proposed and passed the Taft-Hartley Act, which took a big bite out of the pro-labor Wagner Act of 1935. Taft-Hartley let states opt out of big provisions of the Wagner Act, producing so-called right-to-work states and reintroducing cheap labor to the American South, the first states to take advantage of it. Harry Truman vetoed Taft-Hartley, but the Republicans had enough votes to override his veto; and its presence in part made it possible for Ronald Reagan and George W. Bush to so effectively declare war on working people.

One litmus test for politicians—a question you may want to ask—is if they support the repeal of Taft-Hartley. If so, they understand the big picture and support America's having a strong middle class. If not, they're either uninformed or in the pocket of the corporate elite.

NEVER GIVE UP!

On October 29, 1941, during the height of Britain's war with Adolf Hitler, Winston Churchill spoke to the boys at Harrow School, which he'd attended as a child. The boys were terrified by the bombing raids. Each day, it seemed, they read in the papers about another European country's falling to a madman. Churchill, who was battling alcohol, ADHD, and episodic depression along with Hitler, decided to give them a dose of his own internal self-talk, the way he had always successfully pushed himself through the many adversities he had faced in his life.

His words are a good reminder to us as we face the blitzlike destruction wrought on America by nearly three decades of insane con economic, trade, and foreign policies that have left our factories rusting, our neighborhoods devastated, and our people in fear of illness or job loss. "Never give in," Churchill said in a grave voice, his fist in the air, a finger pointed skyward. "Never, never, never, never, in nothing great or small, large or petty, never give in except to convictions of honor and good sense. Never yield to force; never yield to the apparently overwhelming might of the enemy."

We are fighting a war in America for the very heart and soul of our country. But it's a war we can do something about. Don't let yourself be screwed. Speak up, fight back, and never, never yield.

AFTERWORD

GREG PALAST

We're not asking for much: a Social Security check that won't bounce, schools for our kids that won't make them dumber, a fighting chance for a job that will let us take the tykes to Disney World, health insurance, and, when the waters rise, a government that will have some kind of plan to pluck us from the flood.

Fat chance.

Since Thom first wrote this alarm-ringing book, the war has turned severely, senselessly brutal. I'm talking about the class war—and if you're in the middle zone, No Man's Land, well, *good luck, Jack!*

Since Thom's book hit the streets, 38,000 workers at Ford Motor Company lost their jobs. Add that to the Delco Auto Parts bankruptcy, and all of Michigan is busted. In the Bush years, the average annual income in that state declined by $9,000 per family.

You didn't have to move to Michigan to get it in the neck. Average income in the United States has fallen $2,000 per household since the last days of the Bill Clinton presidency.

Hartmann once told me that Thomas Jefferson said his greatest accomplishment was the founding of the University of Virginia—establishing the right of Mr. and Ms. Median Income to a decent, free education. "Universal education," that's what made this nation King of the Planet—a conquest of ideas, ideals, and inventions that no imperial army could have accomplished.

Jefferson considered free universal education so important that he had his university presidency, not the U.S. presidency, carved on his tombstone.

But I think that behind Jefferson's seemingly over-the-top enthusiasm for educating the country was an unstated fear that, unless Americans stayed continually informed, knowledgeable, and alert, we'd end up a nation of knuckleheads and pea-brains ruled by dangerous, pompous pinheads who would take away our rights on the way to taking our wealth.

Jefferson was right: education's the key. I had feared that the 2004 presidential election, recording a Republican plurality, was an intelligence test that America flunked. But by the end of 2006, the Great American Middle rose up in revolt and voted the scoundrels out.

Generally, we've done OK. Franklin D. Roosevelt expanded our Bill of Rights with the Four Freedoms, including a New Deal guaranteeing our economic security. They don't dare take that away—in the open. I know our nation has sometimes fallen into the Bushes, but we always seem to get back up on our hind legs and follow our populist scent back to the True Path.

Of course, the story's not over. Whichever party is in the majority in Congress, it remains a millionaire's club, where average Americans, plucked of their vote, are soon carved into chewable pieces for the corporate carnivores.

Like I say, we're not asking for much: Hartmann's prescriptions to cure America can be summarized on a photo of Laura Bush's fake smile. That's the point. Ultimately, it's not up to the new congressional Democratic majority to save the Great American Middle; it's up to us—to hold them to their promises.

I want you to photocopy Thom's conclusion, "The Road to Victory," and check off each task as you complete it, from joining a union to calling in to a radio talk show.

Then, years from now, when your kids ask you, "What did you do in the class war?" you can point to the list and say, "My share."

Greg Palast is the author of the *New York Times* bestseller *Armed Madhouse: Who's Afraid of Osama Wolf?, China Floats, Bush Sinks, the Scheme to Steal '08, No Child's Behind Left, and Other Dispatches from the Front Lines of the Class War.*

NOTES

References to the thoughts and the words of the Founders were drawn from Thom Hartmann's book *What Would Jefferson Do?* (New York: Crown, 2005).

INTRODUCTION
PROFITS BEFORE PEOPLE

1. *Business Week,* April 21, 2003. *Business Week,* April 18, 2005. U.S. Bureau of the Census, H-6 Table, 2004.

2. "Controversy Continues over Outsourcing Report: Commerce Department 'Disses' Congressional Democrats," *Manufacturing and Technology News,* January 19, 2006. "Jobs Picture: Payrolls up Moderately, but Slack Persists Despite Low Unemployment," Economic Policy Institute, September 2, 2005, http://www.epinet.org/content.cfm/webfeatures_econindicators_jobspict_20050902.

3. Kathy Chu, "For More Companies, 401(k) Becomes Automatic: Employers Freeze Pensions, Push Saving onto Workers," *USA Today,* January 10, 2006, http://www.keepmedia.com/pubs/USATODAY/2006/01/10/1148127?extID=10037&oliID=229.

4. Editorial, "The Pension Deep Freeze," *New York Times,* January 14, 2006.

5. Allstate, 10/4/05.

6. Kaiser Daily Health Policy Report, "Less Than Half of Enrollees Satisfied with Consumer-directed Health Plans, Study Shows," Kaiser Family Foundation, June 14, 2005. U.S. Census 2004, http://www.census.gov.

7. L. Conradt and T. J. Roper, "Group Decision-making in Animals," *Nature* 421 (January 9, 2003): 155–58.

8. James Randerson, "Democracy Beats Despotism in the Animal World," *New Scientist,* January 8, 2003.

9. Paul Craig Roberts, "The True State of the Union: More Deception from the Bush White House," *Counterpunch,* February 1, 2006, http://www.counterpunch.org/roberts02012006.html.

10. Gary Wolfram, "Econ 101: How Do Tax Cuts Work?" January 11, 2006, http://www.freemarketproject.org/commentary/2006/com20060111.asp.

11. Ravi Batra lays this out brilliantly in his book *The Greenspan Fraud* (New York: Palgrave Macmillan, 2005).

12. U.S. Census as reported in The Century Foundation report, "New American Economy: A Rising Tide That Lifts Only Yachts," http://www.tcf.org/publications/economicsinequality/wasow_yachtrc.pdf.

13. David Lazarus, "Plan OK for Rich, Healthy," *San Francisco Chronicle,* February 1, 2006.

14. National Jobs for All Coalition, December 2005 Unemployment Data, http://www.njfac.org.

15. Rob Kelley, "Debt: Consumers Juggle Big Burden," October 10, 2005, http://money.cnn.com/2005/10/07/pf/debt/debtmeasures.

CHAPTER 1

THERE IS NO "FREE" MARKET

1. Gail Russell Chaddock, "U.S. Spending Surges to Historic Level," *Christian Science Monitor,* December 8, 2003.

2. At the time this book was written, Congressman Bernie Sanders of Vermont was running for a seat in the U.S. Senate.

3. Martin Crutsinger, "Slowdown in Red-hot Housing Market Could Spell Trouble for Vulnerable Homeowners," *Associated Press,* February 5, 2006.

4. "An Inside Look: President Bush's 2007 Budget," *NPR.org,* February 6, 2006, http://www.npr.org/templates/story/story.php?storyId=5192631.

5. National Climatic Update Center, December 29, 2005, http://www.ncdc.noaa.gov/oa/climate/research/2005/dec/decemberext2005.html.

6. *St. Petersburg Times,* September 1, 2005.

7. Associated Press, "Death Toll from Katrina Likely Higher Than 1,300," *MSNBC,* February 10, 2006, http://www.msnbc.com/id/11281267.

8. In the long feature "Unacceptable: The Federal Response to Katrina," Walter M. Brasch argues that the response to the Florida hurricanes was purely political and backs his argument with detailed quotes and reference material. September 12, 2005, http://www.dissidentvoice.org/Sept05/Brasch0912.htm.

9. Jonathan S. Landay, Alison Young, and Shannon McCaffrey, "Chertoff Delayed Federal Response, Memo Shows," Knight Ridder newswire, September 13, 2005, http://www.truthout.org/docs_2005/091405A .shtml.

CHAPTER 2

HOW WE THE PEOPLE CREATE THE MIDDLE CLASS

1. Ralph Blumenthal, "As Levi's Work Is Exported, Stress Stays Home," *New York Times,* October 19, 2003.

2. The actual amount is $200,000 in 1944 dollars from Sam Pizzigati, "Shared Sacrifice, Shared Glory," May 28, 2004, http://www.tompaine .com; a conversion chart from 1944 to 2002 dollars can be found at http://www.oregonstate.edu/dept/pol_sci/fac/sahr/cv2002.pdf. Note that the 94 percent marginal tax was a war tax. Roosevelt, however, clearly appreciated a high marginal tax. The marginal tax in 1936 was 79 percent and remained high postwar.

3. David Wessel, "Fed Chief Sets Monetary Policy by Seat-of-the-Pants Approach," *Wall Street Journal,* January 27, 1997.

4. Citizens for Tax Justice, June 12, 2002, http://www.ctj.org/html/ gwb0602.htm.

5. Citizens for Tax Justice, July 2005, citing data from the Institute on Taxation and Economic Policy Tax Model, July 2005, http://www.ctj .org/pdf/gwbdata.pdf.

6. *California Educator,* vol. 9, issue 1, September 2004.

CHAPTER 3

THE RISE OF THE CORPORATOCRACY

1. "Prescriptions and Profit," *60 Minutes* report, August 22, 2004, http:// www.cbsnews.com/stories/2004/03/12/60minutes/main605700.shtml.

2. Drew E. Altman and Larry Levitt, "The Sad History of Health Care Cost Containment," *Health Affairs,* February 23, 2002, http://www .content.healthaffairs.org.

3. Stuart H. Altman et al., "Escalating Health Care Spending: Is It Desirable or Inevitable?" *Health Affairs,* January 8, 2003, http://www .healthaffairs.org:

The 1970s were marked by a number of cost containment efforts by the federal government—the Economic Stabilization Program in 1971–1974, National Health Planning in 1975–1979, and various types of state rate-setting programs—whereas the 1990s were dominated by spending limitations effected through privately managed care plans. In contrast, by the early 1980s most of the governmental regulatory apparatus had been dismantled; and by the late 1980s the few remaining state rate-setting efforts were ended and the market approach of the 1990s had not yet been assembled. One of the authors of this paper has called the 1980s "the decade of halfway competitive markets and ineffective regulation." The years following 1997 indicate a growth rate that is close to what we experienced in the 1980s. In fact, if the current trend continues, growth in health-care spending in the first decade of the twenty-first century could exceed that of the 1980s.

4. Paul Krugman, "Graduates Versus Oligarchs," *New York Times,* February 27, 2006.

5. Ibid., quoting Ian Dew-Becker and Robert Gordon, "Where Did the Productivity Growth Go? Inflation Dynamics and the Distribution of Income" (research paper, Northwestern University, 2005).

6. Matthew Miller and Peter Newcomb, eds., "The 400 Richest Americans," *Forbes,* September 22, 2005.

7. Holly Sklar, "Growing Gulf between Rich and Rest of Us," *CommonDreams.org,* October 3, 2005, http://www.commondreams .org/views05/1003-21.htm.

8. National Center for Education Statistics, using information from the Department of Commerce and the Bureau of Census, cited in Tamara Draught, *Strapped: Why America's 20- and 30-somethings Can't Get Ahead* (New York: Doubleday, 2006).

9. *American Heritage Dictionary* (Boston: Houghton Mifflin, 1983).

CHAPTER 4

THE MYTH OF THE GREEDY FOUNDERS

1. Kevin Phillips, *Wealth and Democracy: A Political History of the American Rich* (New York: Broadway Books, 2002).

2. Bernard Bailyn, *To Begin the World Anew: The Genius and Ambiguities of the American Founders* (New York: Random House, 2003).

3. Forrest McDonald, *We the People: The Economic Origins of the Constitution* (Chicago: University of Chicago Press, 1965).

CHAPTER 6

TAXATION WITHOUT REPRESENTATION

1. *Encyclopaedia Britannica*, 15th ed., s.v. "Boston Tea Party."
2. Bob Herbert, "Let Nike Stay in the Game," *New York Times*, May 6, 2002, http://reclaimdemocracy.org/nike/herbert_let_nike_stay.html.

CHAPTER 8

FDR AND THE ECONOMIC ROYALISTS

1. Rush Limbaugh, "Liberal/Media Action Line Fails on All Fronts," February 17, 2006, http://www.rushlimbaugh.com.

PART III

GOVERNING FOR WE THE PEOPLE

1. Naomi Klein, "Baghdad Year Zero," *Harper's*, September 2004, http://harpers.org/BaghdadYearZero.html.
2. "Iraq's Future Still Going up in Smoke," *Observer*, January 15, 2006, http://observer.guardian.co.uk/business/story/0,,1686490,00.html.
3. Jamie Wilson, "Iraq War Could Cost US over $2 trillion, Says Nobel Prize–winning Economist," *The Guardian*, January 7, 2006, http://www.guardian.co.uk/Iraq/Story/0,2763,1681119,00.html.

CHAPTER 9

TOO IMPORTANT FOR THE PRIVATE SECTOR

1. http://www.goarmy.com/benefits/money_basic_pay.jsp.
2. Michael Scherer, interview by the author, *The Thom Hartmann Radio Program*, Air America Radio, May 4, 2004.
3. Ibid.
4. Ibid.

5. Neil Mackay, "Private Contractors Implicated," *Sunday Herald* (Scotland), May 9, 2004.

6. Human Rights Watch, "Iraq: U.S. Prisoner Abuse Sparks Concerns over War Crimes: Investigation Should Probe Role of Superiors, Private Contractors," May 30, 2004, http://www.hrw.org/english/docs/2004/04/30/iraq8521.htm.

7. Si Kahn and Elizabeth Minnich, *The Fox in the Henhouse: How Privatization Threatens Democracy* (San Francisco: Berrett-Koehler, 2005).

8. Christian Parenti, *Lockdown America: Police and Prisons in the Age of Crisis* (New York: Verso, 2000).

9. Gary E. Johnson, "Bad Investment," *Mother Jones*, July 10, 2001.

10. Vince Besser, "How We Got to 2 Million," *Mother Jones*, July 10, 2001.

11. Johnson, "Bad Investment."

12. Besser, "How We Got to 2 Million."

13. Van Jones, interview by the author, *The Thom Hartmann Radio Program*, Air America Radio, January 3, 2006.

14. Lynn Landes, "Two Voting Companies and Two Brothers," *Online Journal*, April 28, 2004, http://www.onlinejournal.com.

15. Lynn Landes, "Lynn Investigates . . .", http://www.ecotalk.org/VotingMachineCompanies.htm.

16. *Washington Post*, January 13, 1997.

17. Bev Harris, *Black Box Voting: Ballot Tampering in the 21st Century* (Renton, WA: Talion Publishing, 2004).

18. "Senate Contest Tightens: Cleland Clings to Lead over Chambliss," *Atlanta Journal-Constitution*, November 2, 2002.

19. Cox News Service, November 7, 2002.

CHAPTER 10

KNOWLEDGE IS POWER

1. Randi Rhodes, *The Randi Rhodes Show*, Air America Radio, December 15, 2005.

2. I have written a number of books on attention deficit hyperactivity disorder (ADHD), arguing that children with this "diagnosis" do not have something wrong with them but just learn differently.

CHAPTER 11
MEDICINE FOR HEALTH, NOT FOR PROFIT

1. Geeta Anand, "The Big Secret in Health Care: Rationing Is Here," *Wall Street Journal*, September 12, 2003.

2. D. U. Himmelstein and S. Woolhandler, "A National Health Program for the United States: A Physicians' Proposal," *New England Journal of Medicine* 320 (January 12, 1989): 102–108.

CHAPTER 12
THE TRUTH ABOUT THE TRUST FUND

1. Associated Press, "Bush: Social Security Trust Fund 'Just IOUs': President Says, 'There Is No Trust Fund,'" April 6, 2005, http://www .msnbc.msn.com/id/7393649/.

2. Martha Irvine, "Big Voter Turnout Seen Among Young Adults," *USA Today*, November 8, 2004, http://www.usatoday.com/news/ politicselections/2004-11-08-under30_x.htm?POE=NEWISVA.

CHAPTER 14
THE ILLEGAL EMPLOYER PROBLEM

1. A useful table in an online article of the *Christian Science Monitor*, "Illegal Immigrants in the U.S.: How Many Are There?" shows that reliable estimates of the number of illegal immigrants range from 7 million (U.S. Immigration Services) to 20 million (Bear Stearns), http://www.csmonitor.com/2006/0516/p01s02-ussc.html.

2. "Unauthorized Migrants: Numbers and Characteristics," Pew Hispanic Center, June 14, 2005, http://pewhispanic.org/files/reports/46.pdf.

3. "Remittances Reach US$20 Billion in 2005," February 1, 2006, http:// www.eluniversal.com.mx/miami/16816.html.

4. NPR, *All Things Considered*, June 14, 2006.

5. *Hindustan Times,* "Illegal Indians in US Growing Fast," August 19, 2006, http://www.hindustantimes.com/news/181_1772116,00050001.htm.

6. Spencer S. Hsu and Kari Lydersen, "Illegal Hiring Is Rarely Penalized," June 19, 2006, http://www.washingtonpost.com/wp-dyn/content/article/2006/06/18/AR2006061800613.html.

CHAPTER 15

LEVELING THE PLAYING FIELD

1. http://www.census.gov/hhes/http://www/poverty/threshld/thresh04.html.

2. http://www.parentsaction.org/act/family-sick-leave/key-facts.

3. Stephen Franklin and Barbara Rose, "Work 2 Jobs, Have 1 Weary Life," *Chicago Tribune,* September 4, 2005.

4. Jerome Martinez and David Coss, "Higher Pay Good for Santa Fe Workers, Economy," *ABQjournal.com,* September 28, 2005, http://www.abqjournal.com/opinion/guest_columns/393734opinion09-28-05.htm.

5. http://www.faireconomy.org/press/2005/EE2005_pr.html.

CONCLUSION

THE ROAD TO VICTORY

1. ES&S, the second-largest electronic-voting-machine company in the United States, is owned in part by American Information Systems (AIS), which was primarily funded with money from Howard Ahmanson, who also helps finance the Chalcedon Institute, a group which "mandates Christ's dominion over the world." Research provided by Lynn Landes, available at http://www.ecotalk.org/Voting Security.htm.

2. Thomas B. Edsall, "GOP Figure Behind Greens Offer, N.M. Official Says," *Washington Post,* July 12, 2002.

3. Matthew 25:31–40, the parable of the sheep and the goats, is the one place in the New Testament where Jesus says, essentially, "This is what you have to do to get into heaven"—and he says nothing about hating gays or killing off welfare programs to feed the hungry. http://www.biblegateway.com (accessed April 20, 2006):

> **31** When the Son of Man comes in his glory, and all the angels with him, he will sit on his throne in heavenly glory. **32** All the

nations will be gathered before him, and he will separate the people one from another as a shepherd separates the sheep from the goats. 33 He will put the sheep on his right and the goats on his left.

34 Then the King will say to those on his right, "Come, you who are blessed by my Father; take your inheritance, the kingdom prepared for you since the creation of the world. 35 For I was hungry and you gave me something to eat, I was thirsty and you gave me something to drink, I was a stranger and you invited me in, 36 I needed clothes and you clothed me, I was sick and you looked after me, I was in prison and you came to visit me."

37 Then the righteous will answer him, "Lord, when did we see you hungry and feed you, or thirsty and give you something to drink? 38 When did we see you a stranger and invite you in, or needing clothes and clothe you? 39 When did we see you sick or in prison and go to visit you?"

40 The King will reply, "I tell you the truth, whatever you did for one of the least of these brothers of mine, you did for me."

4. Paul Rogat Loeb, *Soul of a Citizen: Living with Conviction in a Cynical Time* (New York: St. Martin's Press, 1999).

INDEX

ACKNOWLEDGMENTS

This is the first book I've written since I started doing live progressive talk radio six hours a day, five days a week. (Several have been published, but all were largely written before I started the radio program.) Because my programs require ten to twelve hours a day of work on weekdays, most of the text was written over the past three years on weekends, much of it as individual essays that first appeared on www.commondreams.org or www.buzzflash.com.

Unlike other books I wrote in the BR (Before-the-Radio-show) era, I couldn't just sit down to write this one straight through as was typical. The result was that it needed considerable editing, stitching together, and in some cases rewriting. For that I am tremendously grateful to Jo Ellen Green Kaiser, who took on an enormous project and in a matter of just a few months spun gold from the straw I'd provided. Perhaps as much as 5 percent of the words in this book are hers, particularly the transitions from chapter to chapter and the translations into prose of some of my on-air rants. Without her this book wouldn't have been possible. Thank you, Jo Ellen!

Special thanks also to the folks at Berrett-Koehler Publishers, who put so much work into transforming the manuscript into the book you're holding in your hands: Johanna Vondeling, Steve Piersanti, Ken Lupoff, and Jeevan Sivasubramaniam in editorial; the design team of Rick Wilson and Dianne Platner; and the marketing team of Maria Jesus Aguilo, Ian Bach, Marina Cook, Mike Crowley, Robin Donovan, Kristen Frantz, Tiffany Lee, and Catherine Lengronne.

Thanks too to my agent, Bill Gladstone.

The book's clean design is the work of the talented Gary Palmatier of Ideas to Images. And special thanks go to Elizabeth von Radics, who performed a brilliant final edit of the text.

And without the help, encouragement, research, and editing work of my wife, Louise Hartmann, this book wouldn't exist. She kept me and the project focused and on track, as she has done for so many other areas of my life. Thank you, Louise!

Finally, I am so grateful to my father, Carl Hartmann, who inspired me with a love of politics and history (even if he *was* a lifelong Republican), and my mother, Helen Jean Hartmann, whose degree in English instilled in me a love of our language and not some inconsiderable proficiency with it. I am indescribably fortunate to have had wonderful parents who were also excellent mentors.

Thom Hartmann

ABOUT THE AUTHOR

National radio host Thom Hartmann is the award-winning, bestselling author of fourteen books currently in print in more than a dozen languages on four continents. Hartmann is also an entrepreneur, an internationally known speaker on culture and communications, and an innovator in the fields of psychiatry, ecology, and economics. The former executive director of a residential treatment program for emotionally disturbed and abused children, he has helped set up hospitals, schools, famine relief programs, and communities for orphaned or blind children in Africa, Australia, Europe, India, Israel, Russia, South America, and the United States. His national radio program, syndicated by Air America Radio, is carried on more than eighty stations across the United States as well as on Sirius Satellite Radio. Hartmann lives in Portland, Oregon, with his wife, Louise, and his attack cat, Higgins. You can find him on the Web at www.thomhartmann.com.

ABOUT BERRETT-KOEHLER PUBLISHERS

Berrett-Koehler is an independent publisher dedicated to an ambitious mission: *Creating a World that Works for All.*

We believe that to truly create a better world, action is needed at all levels—individual, organizational, and societal. At the individual level, our publications help people align their lives with their values and with their aspirations for a better world. At the organizational level, our publications promote progressive leadership and management practices, socially responsible approaches to business, and humane and effective organizations. At the societal level, our publications advance social and economic justice, shared prosperity, sustainability, and new solutions to national and global issues.

A major theme of our publications is "Opening Up New Space." They challenge conventional thinking, introduce new ideas, and foster positive change. Their common quest is changing the underlying beliefs, mindsets, and structures that keep generating the same cycles of problems, no matter who our leaders are or what improvement programs we adopt.

We strive to practice what we preach—to operate our publishing company in line with the ideas in our books. At the core of our approach is *stewardship,* which we define as a deep sense of responsibility to administer the company for the benefit of all of our "stakeholder" groups: authors, customers, employees, investors, service providers, and the communities and environment around us.

We are grateful to the thousands of readers, authors, and other friends of the company who consider themselves to be part of the "BK Community." We hope that you, too, will join us in our mission.

A BK Currents Book

This book is part of our BK Currents series. BK Currents books advance social and economic justice by exploring the critical intersections between business and society. Offering a unique combination of thoughtful analysis and progressive alternatives, BK Currents books promote positive change at the national and global levels. To find out more, visit www.bkcurrents.com.

BE CONNECTED

Visit Our Web Site

Go to www.bkconnection.com to read exclusive previews and excerpts of new books, find detailed information on all Berrett-Koehler titles and authors, browse subject-area libraries of books, and get special discounts.

Subscribe to Our Free E-Newsletter

Be the first to hear about new publications, special discount offers, exclusive articles, news about bestsellers, and more! Get on the list for our free e-newsletter by going to www.bkconnection.com.

Get Quantity Discounts

Berrett-Koehler books are available at quantity discounts for orders of ten or more copies. Please call us toll-free at (800) 929-2929 or e-mail us at bkp.orders@aidcvt.com.

Host a Reading Group

For tips on how to form and carry on a book reading group in your workplace or community, see our Web site at www.bkconnection.com.

Join the BK Community

Thousands of readers of our books have become part of the "BK Community" by participating in events featuring our authors, reviewing draft manuscripts of forthcoming books, spreading the word about their favorite books, and supporting our publishing program in other ways. If you would like to join the BK Community, please contact us at bkcommunity@bkpub.com.